Charitable Giving and Tax Policy

Studies of Policy Reform

Series Editors

Daniel Cohen and Claudia Senik

This series brings new and innovative policy research to the forefront of academic and policy debates.

It addresses the widest range of policies, from macroeconomics to welfare, public finance, trade, migration, and the environment. It hosts collaborative work under the auspices of CEPR and CEPREMAP.

Titles Published in the Series

The Economics of Clusters: Lessons from the French Experience
Gilles Duranton, Philippe Martin, Thierry Mayer, and Florian Mayneris

Cultural Integration of Immigrants in Europe
Edited by Yann Algan, Alberto Bisin, Alan Manning, and Thierry Verdier

Happiness and Economic Growth: Lessons from Developing Countries
Edited by Andrew Clark and Claudia Senik

Charitable Giving and Tax Policy: A Historical and Comparative Perspective
Edited by Gabrielle Fack and Camille Landais

Productivity Puzzles Across Europe
Edited by Philippe Askenazy, Lutz Bellmann, Alex Bryson, and Eva Moreno Galbis

Labour Market and Retirement Interactions
A New Perspective on Employment for Older Workers
Edited by Jean-Olivier Hairault and François Langot

Charitable Giving and Tax Policy

A Historical and Comparative Perspective

Edited by
Gabrielle Fack and Camille Landais

OXFORD
UNIVERSITY PRESS

OXFORD
UNIVERSITY PRESS

Great Clarendon Street, Oxford, OX2 6DP,
United Kingdom

Oxford University Press is a department of the University of Oxford. It furthers the University's objective of excellence in research, scholarship, and education by publishing worldwide. Oxford is a registered trade mark of Oxford University Press in the UK and in certain other countries

First Edition published in 2016

Published in the United States of America by Oxford University Press
198 Madison Avenue, New York, NY 10016, United States of America

British Library Cataloguing in Publication Data
Data available

Library of Congress Control Number: 2015960853

ISBN 978–0–19–872366–0

Acknowledgments

This volume gathers contributions presented at the conference *Altruism and Charitable Giving* jointly organized in May 2012 by the Center for Economic Research and its Applications (CEPREMAP), and the Public Policy group of the Centre for Economic Policy Research (CEPR). The conference was hosted by Paris School of Economics and sponsored by CEPREMAP. The motivation of the conference was to provide a forum for high-quality work in all areas related to the economics of altruism and charitable giving.

The editors would like to thank the authors of the individual chapters, for their contributions and collaborative approach toward developing the chapters. They would also like to thank Thomas Piketty and Emmanuel Saez, co-organizers of the event, and Daniel Cohen, director of CEPREMAP. We also thank all the conference participants for their helpful comments and suggestions. We are also very grateful to those who have been involved in the organization of the event, in particular Catherine Bluchetin and Patricia Guezo at CEPREMAP, Nadine Clarke at CEPR and Sylvain Riffé-Stern at PSE. The views expressed in this volume are those of the authors and do not necessarily represent the views of CEPREMAP, CEPR, or PSE, or of the authors' affiliated organizations.

Contents

List of Figures

List of Figures

List of Tables

List of Contributors

Anthony B. Atkinson, Centennial Professor, LSE, and Honorary Fellow, Nuffield College Oxford

Charles T. Clotfelter, Z. Smith Reynolds Professor of Public Policy and Professor of Economics and Law; Director, Center for the Study of Philanthropy & Voluntarism, Duke University

Gabrielle Fack, Associate Professor of Economics, Université Paris 1 Panthéon Sorbonne and Paris School of Economics

Camille Landais, Associate Professor of Economics, London School of Economics

Kimberley Scharf, Professor of Economics, University of Warwick

Sarah Smith, Professor of Economics, University of Bristol

1

Introduction

Gabrielle Fack & Camille Landais

Even though the level of private philanthropy seems to differ widely across countries, there is little robust quantitative evidence regarding the differentials in private charitable giving across countries and, more importantly, very little consensus on why these differentials exist. Moreover, since the 1990s, these differentials in the level of private contributions to charitable organizations have become a central matter of public policy. Because private charitable contributions finance many socially valuable activities (e.g. education, arts), many governments have tried to boost private philanthropy through various active policy interventions, and this temptation of relying on private contributions to finance the provision of public goods has increased substantially in recent years as fiscal constraints have become tighter. Despite this renewed interest, there is still very little practical and relevant policy guidance that policymakers can find in the economics literature. By providing an original comparative and historical analysis of tax policies towards private philanthropy across different countries, the chapters gathered in this conference volume aim at shedding new light on the determinants of private philanthropy, and ultimately, wish to provide interesting practical insights for improving tax policies towards charitable giving.

In this introduction, we would like to emphasize the interest of focusing on tax policies to study charitable behaviors. Indeed, the advantages of looking at philanthropy through the lens of tax policies are manyfold. First, the long history of tax policies towards charitable giving and private philanthropy is extremely rich and informative about the respective importance of the state and private entities in the provision of public goods. Large and persistent differences in the way private giving is subsidized across countries are also key to understand the role of the charitable sector. The other great advantage of studying tax policies is the availability of tax data. The existence of these special tax treatments for charitable giving has led tax administrations to collect unique information on philanthropic behaviors in the long run in most countries. This information has been regularly published with other exhaustive statistics on income distribution and income composition. These tax statistics therefore provide us with interesting comparative historical information on the level of contributions in the long run. Another great advantage of studying tax policies is that it represents a great laboratory to look into the mechanics of charitable behaviors. The tremendous amount of variations in all dimensions of tax policies (subsidy rate, subsidy mechanism, enforcement policies, direct public provision of public goods, etc.) across countries and over time, but also within country and time across seemingly identical individuals, provides us with many opportunities to identify important behavioral parameters, and test competing models of charitable behaviors. Finally, studying tax policies towards philanthropy is interesting because of its direct practical relevance for policymaking. In most countries, tighter fiscal constraints have called into question the functioning of tax policies towards private charitable giving, but there seems to be little consensus as to how to improve these policies. In fact, the route that goes from positive to normative analysis is far from obvious when it comes to private philanthropy, but the chapters gathered in this volume all aim at making this route a little easier.

We present in the remainder of this introduction all these insightful aspects of the study of tax policies towards private giving. By doing so, we aim to provide an overview of the common themes and a summary of the main findings of all the chapters of the volume. We also take advantage of this introduction to present some original results from our own research project, where we gathered historical tax data on charitable contributions in France, the United States, the United Kingdom, Canada, and Denmark.

1.1 A Rich History of Tax Policies

The comparative history of tax incentives towards private philanthropy reveals important differences in the way the role and mission of the charitable sector have been perceived by the general public as well as by the state. It also offers a striking picture of the various policy tools used over the years and across countries by governments in order to support and/or control private philanthropy. Actual tax systems bear the vivid memory of this long history. We focus primarily on income tax incentives, since almost everywhere they represent the main tool used by governments to subsidize contributions, but also mention other tax incentives when and where they exist.

Today, countries still differ significantly with respect to the nature, the rates and ceiling of their tax incentives for charitable donations.[1] The US system for instance is a deduction from taxable income which is by essence regressive, and the ceiling is very high (50% of income). The French system to the contrary is a non-refundable tax credit, with a very high subsidy rate (66%) and relatively high ceiling. Countries such as the UK have also introduced more sophisticated schemes such as Gift Aid or payroll giving (see Chapter 5). Countries, and this is an important theme of this volume, also widely differ in the level of controls and enforcement of their charitable tax incentives: registration of eligible charities, requirements to qualify as an eligible charity, filing requirements. Tax enforcement of private contributions is for instance still considerably laxer in the United States than in many other countries, such as France, that switched to a system very close to third-party reporting of contributions.

We summarize here the main aspects of this comparative history of tax incentives, country by country. We focus on countries for which we have collected panel data: we compare first the legislation of the US and Canada, where tax incentives for charitable giving were created around World War I. We also talk about the more recent French system, for which we collected data since the 1970s. Lastly, we evoke briefly current tax incentives in Denmark.

1.1.1 *United States*

Tax incentives for charitable giving have existed in the US federal income tax system since 1917, after a first attempt to enact a deduction for gifts to "religious, charitable, scientific, or educational" institutions in 1913 had proved unsuccessful. In practice, the War Revenue Act of 1917 provides a deduction for:

> Contributions or gifts actually made within the year to corporations or associations organized and operated exclusively for religious, charitable, scientific, or educational purposes, or to societies for the prevention of cruelty to children or animals, no part of the net income of which

[1] Readers will find at the end of this introduction a glossary of the various technical terms defining the parameters of the tax system.

> inures to the benefit of any private stockholder or individual, to an amount not in excess of fifteen per centum (15%) of the taxpayer's taxable net income as computed without the benefit of the deduction of such contributions.

From then on, the scope and importance of the deduction from taxable income of charitable donations have increased steadily in the US tax code, under the pressure of the charitable sector and lobbying of some powerful foundations. But as the deduction for charitable giving grew in importance, so did concerns about potential abuses and attempts to curb such abuses. In 1924 for instance, the ceiling of the deduction (at 15% of taxable income) was lifted for very large private contributors, under the condition that in the taxable year and in each of the ten preceding exercises the amount of charitable contributions (plus, for years 1928 and after, the amount of income taxes paid) exceeded 90% of the net income in each such years. But as the practice of claiming deductions for donations made in the past expanded, a tighter control was introduced in 1938 so that contributions were effectively only deductible if paid during the taxable year.

Interestingly, as the isolationist movement grew bigger in the US at the end of the 1930s, so did the concern that the charitable deduction might be subsidizing private contributions to European causes, and from 1938 on, it was enacted that contributions would be deductible only if paid to or for the use of a domestic organization. In 1954, the 15% ceiling was also increased up to 30% for specific gifts to churches and hospitals.

As marginal tax rates reached historical peaks in the late 1940s and 1950s creating a major incentive to donate to charitable causes, reported charitable contributions of the top 0.01% of US taxpayers experienced a tremendous surge. The number of new private foundations also increased significantly during this period. Indeed, foundations experienced very lax control before 1969, and apart from their tax-exempt status, the rules regulating their functioning were nearly nonexistent. Moreover, the audit rates of foundations by the IRS were very low.[2] Therefore, family charitable trusts and private foundations constituted a highly practical vehicle for tax sheltering. Soon, a large number of abuses were reported in a series of reports commissioned by different committees appointed by the US Congress or by the US Department of the Treasury. The Cox Committee Report (1952), the Reece Report (1954), the US Treasury Department report (1965), and

[2] Cf. Peterson (1970).

the Peterson Report (1970) all provide numerous detailed accounts of frauds and abuses. Because of growing public concerns, in 1969, the US Congress passed a tax reform act, TRA69, to better regulate the use of private foundations by high-income taxpayers. The provisions of the new tax law included: the prohibition of "self dealing," defined as activities that benefit foundation managers, officers, substantial contributors, and other foundation insiders; stricter tax rules on unrelated business income (UBI); the establishment of a minimum payout rate as a percentage of investment assets; and the creation of an excise tax on the investment income of private foundations, with an original rate of 4%. Further, while the income ceiling of deductions for public charitable foundations was increased from 30% to 50%, it stayed at 20% for private non-operating foundations, with no possibility for carryover.

Since then, many particular rules and tax reform acts (creation of the alternative minimum tax, rules pertaining to gifts of appreciated stocks, etc.) have affected the subsidies of different types of charitable contribution. TRA1986 for instance, by substantially reducing the effective marginal tax rates paid by top income taxpayers, has greatly reduced tax incentives towards charitable contributions. The other important change to be noted is the 2005 reform of filing requirements of charitable contributions, which tightened the record-keeping requirements for cash and non-cash contributions. However, despite this reform, tax enforcement of private contributions is still considerably lax in the United States compared with all other countries that switched to a system very close to third-party reporting of contributions. In the US, cash contributions under $250 are essentially not monitored.

Overall, the architecture of the income tax deduction has stayed almost unchanged for the past 30 to 40 years. In recent years, the regressivity of the subsidy rate (top income taxpayers facing a higher subsidy because of the progressivity of the income tax schedule) has been criticized, and several proposals have talked about capping the subsidy rate for top income taxpayers or creating a tax credit in lieu of the deduction from taxable income. But all these proposals have stalled after the intensive lobbying of the non-profit sector.

1.1.2 *Canada*

The history of tax incentives for charitable donations in Canada offers an interesting point of comparison with the US (Watson, 1985). An income tax deduction first appeared with the Income War Tax Act in 1917, as Parliament provided unlimited income tax deductions for amounts paid by taxpayers during the year to the Patriotic and Canadian Red Cross Funds, and other patriotic and war funds approved by the Minister. Interestingly, early on, Parliamentarians gave a lot of attention to the possibility that fraudulent unregulated charitable entrepreneurs might take advantage of the deduction and the War Charities Act, which was passed in 1917 both regulated and licensed approved charities. After the war was over, government quickly withdrew (1920) tax incentives that had encouraged donations to wartime charities, even though several attempts were made to revive the tax deduction following the US example.

Eventually, with the outbreak of the Great Depression, a tax deduction of up to 10% of taxable income was reinstated in 1930 and it was specified that only receipted donations would be acceptable for tax deduction. In 1939, charity once again became a priority and the War Charities Act was re-enacted and later replaced by the Income Tax Act (in 1948). Again, tight controls were put in place to curb potential abuses. First, it was noted that there was no master list of charitable organizations available. Each income tax district kept its own. Therefore, from 1948 on, it was enacted that charities wishing to issue receipts for income tax purposes would be required to apply for recognition as charitable organizations on a prescribed form. Also, to prevent wealthy citizens from setting up charitable foundations from which they themselves expected to benefit, in 1950 the government introduced legislation defining a charitable foundation and requiring such foundations to disburse 90% of their annual incomes to charity. Our data show that these tighter controls had important effects on the levels of charitable contributions by top income groups in Canada, compared to the US, were such controls were not put in place until 1969.

Another important change was the introduction of the optional $100 standard deduction in 1957, which applied to charitable donations, medical expenses, and union fees. Because of the relatively tight reporting rules on small gifts (compared with the US), the standard deduction was more appealing than reporting small contributions so that the level of charitable donations reported in tax files declined among lower income taxpayers after 1957, as visible in figure 1.2.

Today, tax incentives have changed to a two-tier tax credit system. The first 200 Canadian dollars of donations produces a 15% rate credit. Gifts in excess of $200 produce a 29% rate credit, with an annual limit on creditable donations of generally 75% of net income.

1.1.3 *France*

France offers an interesting example of a country in which the state has historically tried to limit the development of trusts and foundations. Even though, a deduction from taxable income for charitable donations to some specific foundations has existed in the French Tax code since 1954,[3] its application has been extremely restrictive and the ceiling was originally set at a very low level (0.5% of taxable income). The situation changed in the beginning of the 1970s, when the role of foundations and of the charitable sector began to be recognised and the government set out to encourage its development. The ceiling of the deduction from taxable income was increased, foundations and associations that could qualify for the deduction were no longer restricted and reported contributions started to increase steadily. Interestingly, reporting requirements were limited: taxpayers were only required to keep a receipt of their contributions. This situation changed in 1982 with the requirement to join to a taxpayer's tax form a receipt for any claimed charitable deduction,[4] which resulted in a substantial drop in reported contributions, as shown in figure 1.2.

In 1989, the deduction from taxable income was transformed in a non-refundable tax credit, and over the years, both the tax credit rate and the ceiling have been susbtantially increased in an attempt to boost private philanthropy. Today, the ceiling is set at 20% of taxable income with a possibility to carry-over donations in excess of the ceiling for the next five years. And the tax credit rate is 66%, making it the most generous tax incentive for private contributions among developed countries. Note that the French tax system is also unique in not requiring any registration for charitable organizations to become eligible for the tax deductible donations: any association that can prove to operate for some "general interest," broadly defined, can issue receipts for contributions it receives from individuals.[5] Finally, besides the income tax credit for charitable contributions, the government has also created a wealth tax credit of 66%. Charitable gifts are also exempt from the inheritance tax.

[3] Loi n°54-817 du 14 août 1954, article 11.

[4] Loi 81–1160 art 87.

[5] Note, however, that the creation of foundations is tightly monitored by the state. In order to establish a public utility foundation, the founder must seek authorization (*reconnaissance d'utilité publique*) via a decree issued by the French Ministry of the Interior and the board of the foundation must have at least one representative of the Ministry.

1.1.4 *Denmark*

Denmark is an interesting case. Historically, there is a very strong direct public provision of public goods in Denmark, in all areas from poverty relief to higher education, leaving little room for a large non-profit sector to take care of the provision of public goods in these areas. But in the past 30 years, Denmark has tried to increase the size and scope of its non-profit sector, using tax incentives as a way to encourage private giving. These incentives however have been granted in the context of a very modern tax system with high enforcement level and tight third-party reporting of all claims for tax expenditures. In particular, small contributions below 500 kroners (≈ 60 euros) are not eligible for the charitable giving income tax break. There are today two ways of receiving tax relief in connection with charitable donations to Danish non-profit organizations:

- **Gifts of over DKK 500:** Tax reliefs relating to gifts are calculated annually. Each individual gift must amount to DKK 500 or more in order to be included in the annual statement. In 2009 the maximum tax-deductable amount for one donor was fixed at DKK 14,500.
- **Deed of Gift:** The Deed of Gift is an agreement to donate a specified amount for at least ten years. The entire amount is tax-deductible. The tax deduction is limited to a maximum of 15% of the donor's annual personal income.

1.2 What Can We Learn from Tax Data?

The existence of this long history of tax incentives has one direct advantage for researchers: data availability. The existence of tax incentives induced governments to record information on reported charitable contributions, that can now be used to analyze the long run evolution of private philanthropy across countries.

Until now, comparative statistics on charitable behaviors across countries were usually drawn from survey data. Survey evidence is interesting, but experience proves that its reliability for international comparisons can be limited, because of such issues as self-declaration of contributions, small sample sizes in most surveys, framing in the questions, and other common methodological issues. Figure 1.1 shows the fraction of individuals reporting being a donor to charitable causes by country in the European Social Survey for European countries and

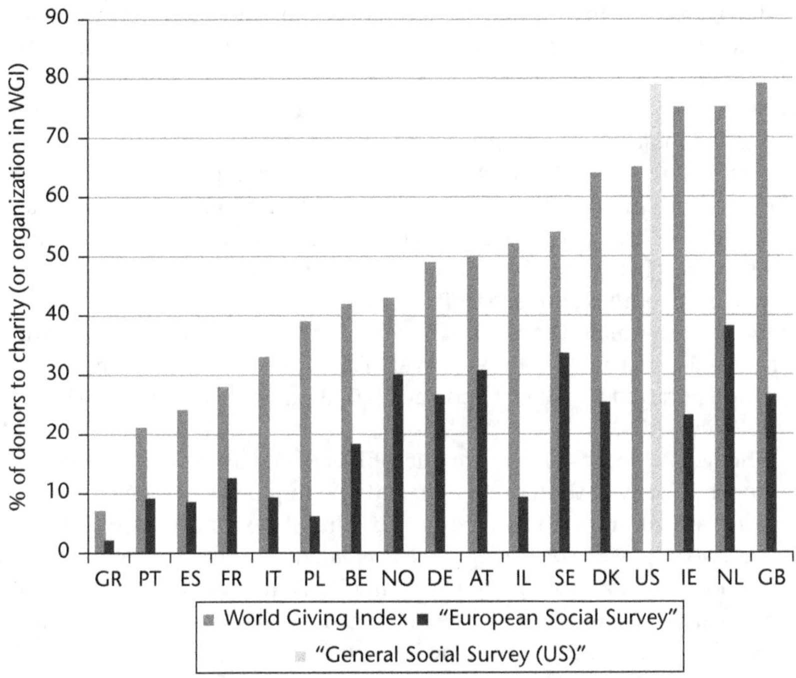

Figure 1.1 Fraction of the Population Reporting Charitable Contributions in Different Surveys

Sources: Author's computation from European Social Survey (2002) and General Social Survey for the US (2002) as well as from the World Giving Index (2011).

General Social Survey for the US (in 2002) and compares it with the recently created World Giving Index (WGI) (2011).[6] Both levels and rankings differ substantially across surveys for some countries such as the United Kingdom. One reason for this discrepancy is that the definition of a gift to charity varies from one survey to another.[7] Moreover, surveys typically lack consistency over time, limiting researchers' ability to exploit policy variations in order to identify relevant behavioral parameters and compare them across countries.

[6] The data is from Gallup's Worldview World Poll, conducted on 153 countries. See <https://www.cafonline.org/publications/2011-publications/world-giving-index-2011.aspx>.

[7] ESS asks whether the respondent donated money to specific types of charities (e.g. humanitarian organization, religious/church organization, ...), whereas GSS and WGI have a more general question about giving money to charity.

To overcome the limitations of survey data, and shed new light on charitable behaviors over time and across countries, we have collected historical tax data in five countries, using information available in tax returns from charitable giving deductions/tax credits. Our data comes from two major types of source.

First, we used yearly tabulations of income, composition of income and amounts of deductions/tax credits by income level produced by tax administrations of these five countries since the creation of the income tax system. This gives us information on total contributions reported by taxpayers over time. But the fruitful information of these tables can also serve to extrapolate the level of income, the income composition and the level of charitable giving for every fractile of top incomes following methods drafted in Piketty and Saez (2003) and discussed in Atkinson and Piketty (2007).

The second source of data are microfiles created by tax administration from large (or even sometimes exhaustive) sample of taxpayers and containing all the information from individuals' tax returns. Combining these two types of sources, we have created a unique dataset on the evolution of charitable giving in Canada, Denmark, France, and the United States. This dataset is the first consistent comparative source on charitable contributions over the long run across these countries.

There are nevertheless important limitations of the data that are important to keep in mind. Filing and reporting requirements for taxpayers have changed over time and vary across countries. The level of enforcement of tax incentives for charitable contributions varies also significantly across countries and over time.

Variation in filing requirements is probably the most important source of difficulty for historical and international comparisons introduced by the tax data. At the very beginning of the twentieth century for instance, only a small fraction of the population filed tax returns, so little is known of the income and charitable donations of individuals who did not file a return. Only since the mid-1940s did the vast majority of individuals in all five countries systematically file returns. The reporting requirements for small contributions vary also considerably across countries. In Denmark for instance, donations under 500 Danish kroners are not deductible whereas in the US, individuals can deduct small gifts without joining a receipt to their tax return.

Similarly, certain countries offer to their taxpayers a choice between taking itemized deductions (including charity), or a standard deduction. This has been the case in the United States ever since 1944, or in Canada since 1957. As a result, tax return data in the US or in Canada only provides information on the charitable donations of people who choose to itemize their deductions, which introduces a bias in the estimates of overall donations. The reason is that the decision to itemize is endogenously related to the size of one's charitable donation. People with unusually large charitable donations are more likely to itemize than people with similar characteristics but with smaller itemized deductions, because the former group is more likely to have itemized deductions that exceed the standard deduction. The extent to which this biases estimates of mean charitable donations by income class and year varies greatly by income class and by year. The bias is much more extreme at lower income levels, because people with lower incomes are far less likely than higher-income people to have non-charitable itemized deductions large enough to exceed the standard deduction, and those that do not tend to have non-charitable itemized deductions tend to be further below the standard deduction threshold. Thus, for low- and middle-income people, data on charitable donations from US or Canadian tax return data is really only representative of people who are at the extreme right-end tail of the generosity distribution. By contrast, higher income people are far more likely than lower-income people to have non-charitable itemized deductions that exceed the standard deduction, so that statistics on charitable donations by high-income itemizers will be representative of a much broader slice of the generosity distribution.

These differences in filing and reporting requirements significantly affect the fraction of small contributions reported to the tax administration, and therefore have an important effect on aggregate figures of reported contributions, as shown in figure 1.2. To alleviate this issue, two solutions can be implemented.

First, it is sometimes possible to correct for the bias introduced by itemization using microdata. When microdata is available (for years 1960 and after in the United States for instance), one can compute contributions as a fraction of total income for exogenous itemizers in each income group, where exogenous itemizers are defined as individuals who have non-charitable itemized deductions that exceed the standard deduction. One can then use these observations to construct a correction factor to adjust the series when no microdata is available. The correction factor can be income-group specific (to take care of the fact that the itemization issue is likely to be a little more severe for individuals in the lower half of the top decile of richest taxpayers). The correction factor can also be made dependent on the ratio of the standard deduction to the average income in the income group, to take care of the fact that as the standard deduction increases (as a fraction

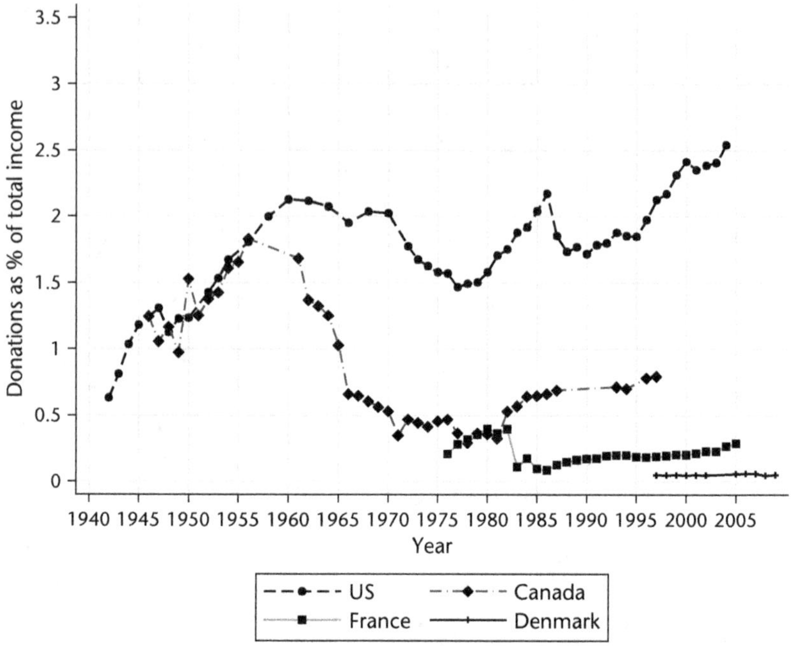

Figure 1.2 Reported Donations as a Fraction of Total Income for the Top 10% of Taxpayers across Countries

Sources: Authors' computation from income tax statistics. See text for details.

of income), the probability to itemization will decrease for any level of contributions.

A second, more straightforward way of alleviating the issue is to focus on top income groups, defined as individuals in the top 10% of taxpayers with the highest gross income. The advantage of focusing on top income groups is that they represent a population with high filing and reporting rates throughout the twentieth century, enabling consistent comparisons over time and across countries.[8]

Figures 1.2, 1.3, and 1.4 summarize the key learnings from tax sources on the long-run evolution of private charitable contributions. First, total reported charitable contributions as a fraction of total gross

[8] Note that some countries enable charitable deduction through the estate tax system as well. Some individuals may also use corporate income to operate charitable contributions. Our estimates of total contributions of top incomes might therefore underestimate total private philanthropy of the very wealthy. However, the tax incentives for charitable donations being almost always higher in the individual income tax system, reported contributions through the individual income tax always dwarf reported contributions through the estate or the corporate income tax.

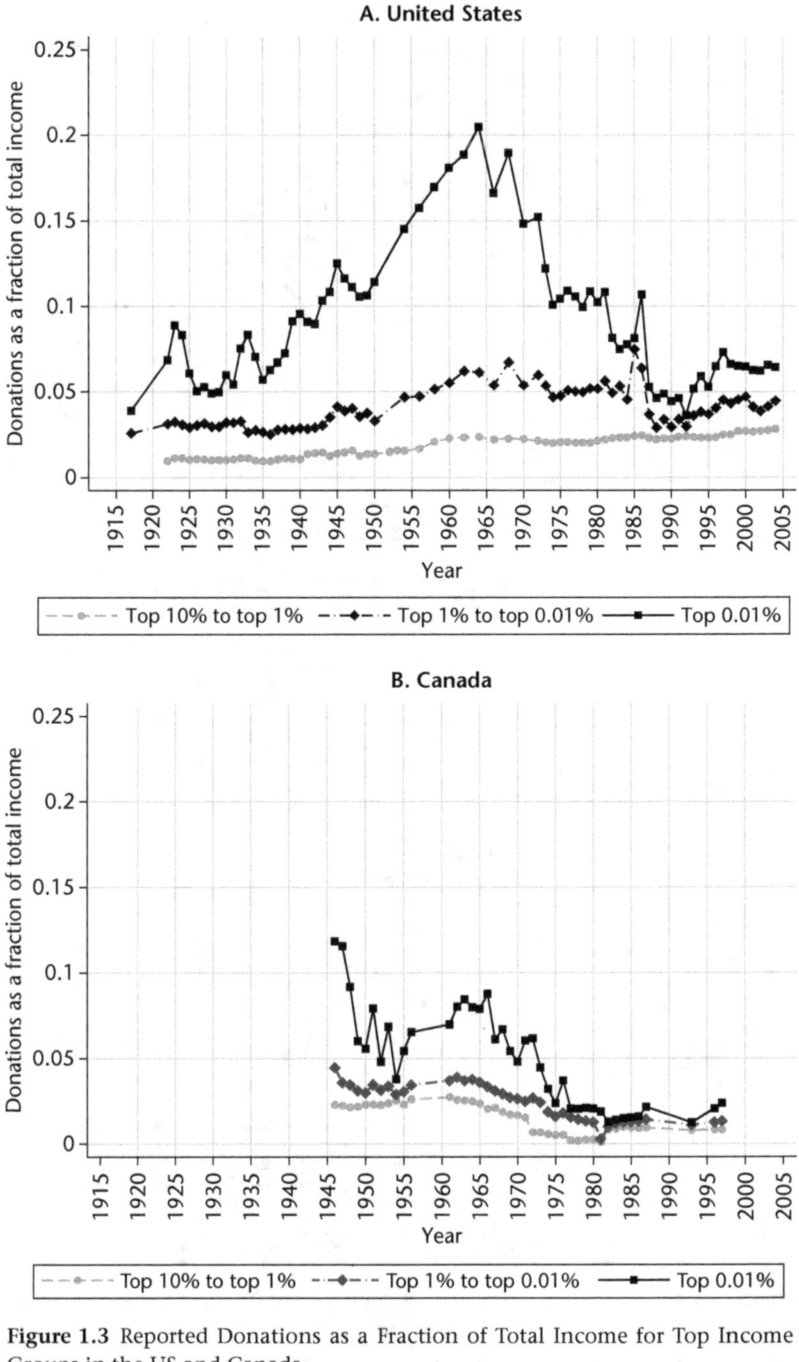

Figure 1.3 Reported Donations as a Fraction of Total Income for Top Income Groups in the US and Canada

Notes: Both panels show reported donations for top income groups as a fraction of total income excluding capital gains.

Sources: Authors' computation from income tax statistics.

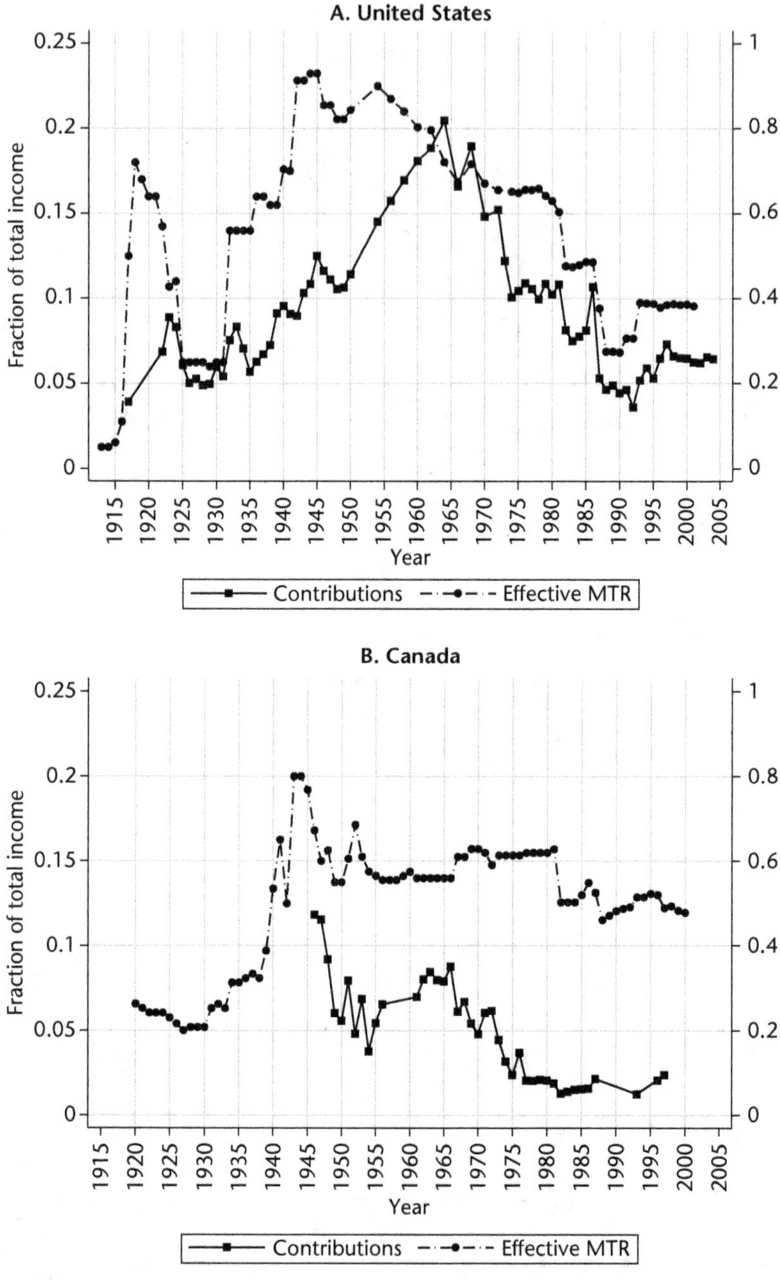

Figure 1.4 Effective Marginal Tax Rates and Reported Donations as a Fraction of Total Income for Top 0.01% of Richest Taxpayers in the US and Canada

Notes: Both panels show reported donations for top income groups as a fraction of total income excluding capital gains. Effective marginal tax rates series for Canada come from Saez and Veall (2005), and for the US come from authors' historical tax simulator before 1960 and NBER TAXSIM after 1960.

Sources: Authors' computation from income tax statistics.

income are significantly higher in the US than in all other countries, and historically, this has always been the case. France and Denmark have aggregate levels of reported contributions that are around ten times lower. Canada is an interesting case: in the 1940s and first half of the 1950s, aggregate levels of reported contributions in Canada were on par with that of the US, but then declined steadily, and have been around a third of the US figures since the 1960s. Differences in reporting requirements and tax enforcement might explain a lot of the evolution of aggregate reported contributions displayed in figure 1.2. First, the ability to report small contributions differ widely across countries. Denmark for instance does not allow deduction of contributions below 500 kroners. Second, requirements to join the receipts also differ. In France for instance, joining receipts to one's tax return was not required before 1983, which explains the huge drop in charitable contributions between 1982 and 1983. In Canada, the introduction of a standard deduction and tight controls on small contributions and the operation of charitable organizations as explained above, explain the decline in aggregate contributions compared with the US.

When focusing on top income groups, huge differences persist across countries and over time. In figure 1.3, we plot the evolution of donations as a fraction of total income (excluding capital gains) for the top 10 to 1%, top 1 to 0.01% and top 0.01% of taxpayers in the US and in Canada. In the mid-1940s, donations of top income groups were almost similar in both countries, but surged throughout the 1950s in the US, while they declined in Canada. Today, charitable donations of the top 0.01% of taxpayers are two times higher in the US than in Canada.

The chapters in this volume try to investigate the main sources that drive these huge differentials in giving.

One often cited explanation for the large differences in charitable giving across countries relates to differences in the level of income inequality across countries, and in particular the large top income shares in English-speaking countries compared with continental Europe. It is true for instance that real disposable incomes of people in the top 10% of the income distribution increased dramatically since the 1970s in the United States. This should have contributed to a steady increase in charitable contributions if charitable contributions is a normal good. It is nevertheless fascinating that Canada did not experience a similar surge in charitable contributions over the same period, while top income shares have nevertheless followed patterns comparable to the United States. Furthermore, as shown in figure 1.4, for taxpayers belonging to the top 0.01% income group in the United States, contributions as a fraction of income reached a peak between the 1950s and 1960s, when their total income share was at an historic low. This evidence casts doubts on the ability of income inequality alone to explain historical and cross-country evolutions in total reported contributions displayed in figure 1.2.

An important contribution of our original dataset is to show that, cultural explanations *stricto sensu*—or more generally, idiosyncratic country-specific characteristics—even though they may be important in explaining variations across countries (France vs the US for instance), seem ill-equipped to explain the large variations over time in Canada or in the US. In this volume, we pay particular attention to the impact of public policies, and especially tax policies, in explaining these differentials. We investigate two specific aspects of tax policies: first the generosity of the incentives, and second the enforcement of these incentives. In figure 1.4, for instance we plot the evolution of charitable donations by the top 0.01% of taxpayers in Canada and the US against the evolution of their effective marginal tax rate (which determines the "price" of their donations). Interestingly, top effective marginal tax rates were around 20 percentage points lower in Canada than in the US in the 1950s. Another important feature of tax policies towards philanthropy that we develop in this volume is enforcement. As noted, Canada did put in place very early on strict rules concerning the operation of charitable organisations and their eligibility to the charitable deduction, while rules were much laxer in the United States.

The chapters in this book investigate more precisely the role of tax incentives on charitable giving, from a normative and a positive perspective.

1.3 Behavioral Responses to Tax Policies

1.3.1 *Price Elasticities*

The positive analysis of the effect of tax incentives focuses on the behavioral responses to taxation. The most discussed parameter in this literature is the price elasticity of giving, which measures how taxpayer's reported charitable contributions change as the "price of giving" changes due to changes tax incentives: for example, an elasticity of -1 means that a 1% decline in the tax price leads to a 1% increase in contributions. The responsiveness of taxpayers conditions the optimality of such tax incentives and most authors have focused on the "unit elasticity rule," which states that tax incentives are efficient if the price elasticity of giving is equal or larger than one in absolute value. Indeed, in a simple model where the government's objective is to maximize charitable contributions, with an elasticity larger than one in absolute value, the loss of tax revenue generated by an increase in tax deductions is more than compensated by an increase in charitable contributions. So far, as discussed in Chapters 3 and 4, the empirical literature trying to estimate this elasticity has produced mixed results. In Chapter 4, we use our long panel from the US to provide new estimates of the responsiveness of charitable giving among the top 10% of taxpayers. The main advantage of our dataset is that it gives us the opportunity to exploit both large increases and decreases in marginal tax rates for higher income households over the twentieth century. We do find a long term elasticity lower than one in absolute value, except for households at the very top of the income distribution, who appear to be more responsive to tax incentives.

Chapters 4 and 5, however, show that despite the importance of the estimation of the price elasticity of charitable giving in the literature, this single parameter appears to be insufficient to design optimal tax incentives.

1.3.2 *Matching vs Rebate*

Kimberley Scharf and Sarah Smith show in Chapter 5 that not only the level of the tax incentive matters, but also its framing. Behavioral studies provide evidence that individuals respond differently to incentives when they are framed as a match or a rebate. In Chapter 5, Smith and Scharf hypothesize that some behaviors such as "rational inattention" might explain this discrepancy and analyze further how this may affect UK tax policy. The UK tax incentive system, which already has both matching and rebate components, constitutes an ideal setting to investigate more precisely whether individuals respond differently to similar changes in tax incentives when they are framed differently. Smith and Scharf indeed show with survey data that individuals tend to be more responsive to changes in matches, and they discuss how this may impact the optimal tax policy.

1.3.3 *Tax Cheating*

Chapter 4 also points out the limitations of the unit elasticity rule in the presence of tax cheating. As we already highlighted in our comparison of the existing incentives among countries, tax enforcement varies a lot across countries. We show in chapter 4 that, in the presence of tax cheating, the price elasticity of reported contributions is no longer a sufficient statistic to assess the optimality of tax incentives. In this chapter, we also unveil the existence of substantial tax evasion carried out through charitable deductions using a natural experiment on tax enforcement in the US. We finally discuss how optimal tax policies for charitable contributions can be reassessed in the presence of tax cheating.

1.4 Welfare and Policy Implications

The chapter gathered in this volume try to inform us about welfare and to improve our ability to design tax policies. They do so essentially along three dimensions.

First, by asking the question "why do people contribute to public goods?", which is the natural starting point of all welfare analysis. Standard analysis has always assumed a mixture of "warm-glow" and public good motives to explain the important level of charitable contributions observed in the data. But as explained by Anthony Atkinson in Chapter 2, this mixture of motives, although it improves the ability of the model to explain empirical facts about giving, creates problems when it comes to welfare analysis: when aggregating people's preferences, shall the warm-glow or other individual motives be incorporated in the social welfare function, or is it double-counting, as argued by Diamond (2006)? Another complication pointed out in this volume is the presence of "behavioral biases" which affect the way people's giving behaviors react to seemingly equivalent subsidy-schemes, like the rebate vs matching example in the experiment presented by Scharf and Smith in Chapter 5. These observations show that our understanding of the motivation behind charitable giving, which should be at the core of the design of optimal tax policies towards private philanthropy, is still very incomplete.

The second important dimension highlighted in this volume relates to the definition of what constitutes a public good for the tax administration. As developed by Charles Clotfelter in Chapter 3, many contributions eligible for the charitable deduction in the US do indeed finance goods that are partly public and partly private. This of course creates important redistribution issues when it comes to evaluate the welfare impact of the charitable deduction. And shows how the definition of what constitutes a charitable purpose (and therefore what types of gifts and of organizations qualify for the charitable deduction) is even more central to the definition of the optimal tax policy than the level of the incentive itself.

A final aspect and rather original dimension of this volume is to underline the importance of the level of enforcement of tax policies towards private philanthropy. By highlighting that a non-trivial fraction of reported charitable contributions may be driven by tax sheltering purposes when enforcement regimes are lax, Chapter 4 reminds us that high price elasticities of giving might be meaningless for welfare analysis when driven by tax avoidance motives.

1.5 Organization of the Volume

The remainder of the volume is organized as follows.

In the second chapter of this volume, Anthony B. Atkinson offers a general overview of the deep and intricate relationships between altruism and economics. Atkinson tackles several important questions related to the modeling of charitable giving that have been overlooked in most empirical and theoretical work. First, he confronts the usual modeling of charitable giving behavior to a specific case of charitable donation: giving overseas. He argues that, in order to explain this specific type of charitable giving, one has to depart from the traditional view that charitable gifts are either due to altruistic or warm-glow motives. He proposes instead the "identification model" in order to take into account that individuals may give without expecting a direct benefit from their gift nor from the services that are provided by the charity, but rather have a concern for the well-being of others. This poses the normative question on whether and how we should take into account this "identification" motive in the social welfare function, when determining the optimal policy. Atkinson also argues that it is important to adopt a lifetime approach to the analysis of charitable giving. Existing studies have generally focused on the analysis of charitable behavior over a limited period of time, whereas charitable giving decisions are taken over the lifetime. A comprehensive analysis should analyze jointly the motives for giving in the course of a lifetime and at death.

In the following chapter of this volume, Charles T. Clotfelter offers a thorough portrait of tax policy towards private charitable giving in the US. The United States, by almost all standards, stand out as the country with the largest and most active charitable sector. Clotfelter begins by explaining the historical and cultural roots of this American exceptionalism. He then offers a detailed account of the tax rules pertaining to charitable giving in the US. He then turns to the critical importance of a tiny fraction of very wealthy individuals in the functioning of the charitable tax deduction, and analyzes the issues this creates for welfare and redistribution. Finally, Clotfelter discusses the most recent proposals regarding tax incentives for charitable giving, and especially, the pros and cons of capping the subsidy rate for top income taxpayers, as envisaged by the Obama administration.

In Chapter 4, we analyze the US tax policy for charitable giving in a more historical perspective. Using US tabulated tax statistics and micro tax data, we build long-term series of contributions and marginal tax rates for the top US income groups since 1917 and document a drastic surge in contributions by the very wealthy in the 1945–1969 period. We then use those series to obtain robust estimates of the standard price elasticity of reported charitable contributions. We also show how part of this high sensitivity of reported contributions to marginal tax rates may be due to the very lax enforcement regime of the charitable deduction before 1969. We use the 1969 tightening of rules for contributions to private foundations in the United States in a difference-in-difference approach to document sizeable responses to the tax enforcement regime, implying that the share of tax-sheltering motive in total reported contributions by the very wealthy may be significant. We also develop a model of charitable contributions in the presence of "cheating" contributions and present formulas for the optimality of tax subsidies for contributions to discuss the policy implications of our empirical findings. In addition to the standard price elasticity of reported charitable contributions, two new parameters appear in the formulas: the share of "cheating" contributions in total reported contributions and the price elasticity of "cheating" contributions. Simple calibrations based on our estimates show that the issue of tax sheltering through charitable contributions is a first-order consideration for the design of optimal subsidies.

Finally, in Chapter 5, Kimberley Scharf and Sarah Smith give an interesting analysis of the UK system of tax incentives for charitable giving. They pay particular attention to how the framing of the tax incentive affects individual giving behaviors. The UK tax incentive system has both a matching and a rebate component. Smith and Scharf use this ideal setting to investigate more precisely whether individuals respond differently to similar changes in tax incentives when they are framed differently. They show that individuals are indeed more responsive to price variations in a matching system than in a rebate system. This empirical evidence demonstrates that price elasticities are fundamentally contextual statistics, which depend a lot on the institutional details of the tax system. The authors then discuss the consequences of their empirical findings for the optimal design of tax incentives.

1.6 Glossary

- **Ceiling**: the maximum amount that individuals can claim for a deduction or a tax credit. It is usually defined as a fraction of taxable income.
- **Deduction from taxable income**: tax incentive consisting in allowing individuals to reduce the amount of their taxable income by deducting specific expenditures from their total income. The marginal incentive of making a contribution in such a system will directly depend on the marginal income tax rate of the taxpayer. If the marginal tax rate faced by the taxpayer is τ, the marginal price of contribution will be $1 - \tau$. In others words, the higher one's marginal tax rate τ, the lower the price of making contributions.
- **Non-refundable tax credit**: a tax credit is a reduction of one's tax liability. It is usually granted conditional on meeting some requirements. A tax credit for charitable contributions will typically consist in granting a reduction in one's tax liability equal to a fraction t of the contributions g incurred by the taxpayer. When the tax credit is non-refundable, individuals will get a payment of equal to $\min(t \cdot g, T)$, where T is the taxpayer's initial tax liability.
- **Match**: incentive consisting in topping up an individual's contribution by an additional amount, usually expressed as a fraction of the original contribution.
- **Price elasticity of contributions**: the elasticity measures how taxpayers reported charitable contributions change (in percentage term) as the price of giving varies by one percent due to changes tax incentives. For example, an elasticity of -1 means that a 1% decline in the tax price leads to a 1% increase in contributions.
- **Rebate**: incentive consisting in reducing the price of a contribution by "rebating" the donor a fraction of her contribution.
- **Refundable tax credit**: a tax credit is a reduction of one's tax liability. It is usually granted conditional on meeting some requirements. A tax credit for charitable contributions will typically consist in granting a reduction in one's tax liability equal to a fraction t of the contributions g incurred by the taxpayer. When the tax credit is refundable, individuals will get a payment of $t \cdot g$ irrespective of whether $t \cdot g$ is smaller or larger than the taxpayer's actual tax liability.

References

Atkinson, Anthony B. and Thomas Piketty, eds (2007). *Top Incomes over the Twentieth Century: A Contrast between European and English-Speaking Countries* (Oxford: Oxford University Press).

Diamond, Peter, (2006). "Optimal Tax Treatment of Private Contributions for Public Goods with and Without Warm Glow Preferences," *Journal of Public Economics, 90* (4–5), 897–919.

Peterson, P. (1970). *Foundations, Private Giving and Public Policy: Report and Recommendations of the Commission on Foundations and Private Philanthropy* (Chicago: University of Chicago Press).

Piketty, Thomas and Emmanuel Saez, (2003). "Income Inequality in the United States, 1913–1998," *Quarterly Journal of Economics, 118* (1), 1–41.

Saez, Emmanuel and Michael R. Veall, (2005). "The Evolution of High Incomes in Northern America: Lessons from Canadian Evidence," *American Economic Review, 95* (3).

Watson, Rod, (1985). "Charity and the Canadian Income Tax: An Erratic History," *The Philanthropist, 5* (1), 3–21.

2

Charitable Giving and Economics

Anthony B. Atkinson

2.1 Introduction

Charitable giving is an important subject. Many governments see enhanced charitable giving as an alternative to public spending—an alternative that is increasingly attractive as fiscal constraints become tighter. Charitable giving has also become of considerable interest to economists. The rich and substantial literature over recent decades means that it now constitutes a significant sub-field of the discipline, recognized in major reviews such as the *Handbook of the Economics of Giving, Altruism and Reciprocity* (Kolm and Ythier, 2006). It is however essential that it should not become too divorced from the mainstream of economics. In this chapter, I argue that the study of charitable giving has important implications for the development of economics—both positive and normative economics.

In making this argument, I shall take a specific case study that illustrates well a number of the general issues. The case study is of giving for overseas development. In the United Kingdom (UK), charitable donations by individuals for overseas development are substantial. Charities focusing on overseas development and emergency relief received nearly £1 billion in donations, bequests, and other forms of "voluntary income" in 2004–5 (Charities Aid Foundation, 2006), which was equal to about a quarter of the figure for Official Development Assistance (ODA) in that year. Over a quarter of a century from 1978, giving for development in the UK increased more than sixfold in real terms (Atkinson et al., 2012, Figure 2). Focusing on this case study allows us to identify a number of key issues for the economic analysis of charitable giving in general, and, indeed, for economics more broadly.

The first section of the chapter reconsiders the motives for charitable giving within the framework of utility maximization. The literature has typically assumed the utility to take two main alternative forms (see Andreoni, 2006). The first is that utility is derived from the achieved results of the gift, referred to as the "public good" motive; the second is that utility is derived directly from the act of giving, which has come to be known as the "warm-glow" motive. In Section 2.2, I argue, following Atkinson (2009) that neither of these formulations is fully appropriate for the explanation of giving to development charities, and propose a new formulation, the "identification" approach, that blends the scale of the warm-glow approach with the results focus of the public goods formulation. In putting this forward, I am not suggesting that the identification approach is of wider validity, but rather that the development of microeconomic models needs to consider the specific application and impose the structure appropriate to the application. It is not sufficient to write a general utility function; nor is it adequate to take over a function applied elsewhere. We need to drill down to the essentials of the problem.

Giving for development takes place in the course of the lifetime and at death in the form of bequests. The modeling of giving has therefore to adopt a lifetime approach, and to this end the standard model of life-cycle savings has been commonly employed (see, for example, Watson, 1984). Following the strategy of "drilling down", we need to consider the specific features of charitable giving. These are the subject of Section 2.3. The first is that many people give nothing at a particular date or leave no charitable bequests. In contrast to much microeconomic theory, where corner solutions are often ignored, they should receive particular attention when studying charitable giving, since time may be of the essence. But we have also to consider the challenges that have been made to the underlying model, notably from recent advances in behavioral economics and from experimental evidence (see, for example, the survey of field experiments by DellaVigna, 2009). With a wide range of possible factors affecting intertemporal behavior, the need for more structure is even more apparent, and this is illustrated by reference to the different stages involved in the decision to make a charitable bequest.

In the first two sections, I am concerned with the positive theory of charitable giving. In Section 2.4, I turn to the normative questions and the challenges for welfare economics. These are twofold. First, the existence of individual concern for charitable objects raises the issue as to how such individual concerns should enter the social welfare function. Should, as some writers have argued, warm-glow preferences be simply disregarded in the social evaluation? Secondly, the case study considered here raises the issue of the global reach of the social welfare function—an issue that transcends charitable giving and touches all policy that has implications beyond national boundaries. The final section summarises the conclusions for the economics of charitable giving—and for economics more generally.

2.2 The Motives for Giving

If we denote charitable donations by D and consumption by C, then a household may be represented as maximising U(C,D) subject to a budget constraint, where the constraint will reflect such considerations as income tax exemptions for donations that influence the "price" of giving. Much of the literature has been concerned with the impact on the level of giving of variations in the price. Where utility is assumed to be derived directly from the act of giving—the "warm-glow" hypothesis—the formulation is complete. All that is required is the specification of the form of the utility function.

Pure warm-glow models, however, assume that the donor is completely unconcerned with the use made of the gift and with the effectiveness of charitable activity. This assumption is unappealing in the case of giving for overseas development, where a key role is played by issues of "effectiveness." A reason frequently advanced for not giving is that the money is wasted: it disappears in administrative costs or is lost in corruption. Qualitative research in the UK (Atkinson and Eastwood, 2007) indicates the role played by negative stories about misgovernment in dissuading people from giving for development. The warm-glow model allows no scope for such considerations.

This objection does not apply to the second formulation—the public goods motive—where the donor is assumed to be concerned with the achieved results of the gift. Assuming that the utility function is additively separable in the two components, we can write utility as U(C) + V(G[D]), where G[D] is the level of the public good. U and V are assumed to be non-decreasing, concave functions, but these assumptions on their own are not sufficient. We have to provide more structure. Where charitable contributions support public goods of a conventional kind, such as a hospice or public radio, the function V represents the valuation placed on the resulting services. In the case of giving for development, however, the motive is more one of extended "sympathy." As was described by Sen in his analysis of worker co-operatives, "families are not necessarily indifferent to the happiness of other families... and their notion of 'social welfare' takes into account the utility of other families" (1966, p. 363). The utility function may then be written as

$$U(C) + \delta r U(G[D]) \tag{2.1}$$

where δ captures the fact that the degree of sympathy may be incomplete or zero ($0 \leq \delta \leq 1$) and r denotes the number of recipients. The case where δ is between 0 and 1 has been colorfully described by Edgeworth: "between the frozen pole of egoism and the tropical expanse of utilitarianism [there is] the position of one for whom in a calm moment his neighbour's happiness as compared with his own neither counts for nothing, nor 'counts for one' but counts for a fraction" (1881, p. 102). In planning its giving, the household has to take a view about the contribution that its own donation, D, makes to the outcome. The outcome depends on the contributions of others, including, in the present case, ODA. As has been widely recognized in the literature, the problem with the public goods motive is that there is an incentive to free-ride, attenuated only to the extent that contributors expect that increases in their own giving will stimulate others to give more (Jones and Posnett, 1993, p. 135).

A second feature of giving for development is that, in contrast to the worker co-operative, the number of recipients is likely to be large. This calls into question the formulation (1), since, as r becomes large, the maximand is dominated by the second term. There would be a sum over 1 donor and millions of recipients. More reasonable would be to assume that the donor is concerned with the average level of well-being of recipients (removing the variable r in equation (1)). But we have also to allow for the fact that the number of potential donors is large. Large numbers of donors means that people are less likely to assume that their own giving will stimulate other donors and that the individual donors are more likely to free-ride (Atkinson, 2009, p. 649). For these reasons, as Sugden argued many years ago, "the public good theory of philanthropy is untenable as an explanation of the behavior of those people who contribute to large charities" (Sugden, 1982, p. 348). In the case of development charities, the public goods model does not for this reason provide a satisfactory basis for the explanation of individual giving.

On their own, the two standard models do not apply to the case of giving for development, but a combination of the two approaches is more promising. In the "identification model" (Atkinson, 2009), the donor is assumed to be concerned with the impact on the living standards of the recipients, but the donor does not regard D as being divided among millions of potential recipients. Donors are assumed to visualize a small number (m) of recipients aided only by them. Such a visualization is commonly promoted by development charities, and some charities have sought indeed to build explicit links between donors and recipients. Such a utility function may be written as (assuming that the transfer is equally divided among the m visualized recipients):

$$U(C) + \delta m \cdot U(Y_0 + (1 - l)D/m) \tag{2.2}$$

where the living standard of the recipients would be Y_0 in the absence of assistance and there is a leakage of a proportion l from the charitable transfer. The condition for a charitable gift to be made is that

$$\delta(1 - l) \cdot U'(Y_0) > p \cdot U'(C) \tag{2.3}$$

where p is the price of giving (for example $(1 - \tau)$ in the case where donation are tax-deductible and τ is the marginal tax rate). As discussed further below, the corner condition is of particular interest since it determines the proportion making a charitable gift. Where, for instance, people differ in their degree of extended sympathy, δ then the proportion making a gift is $1 - F(\delta^*)$, where F is the cumulative distribution of δ and δ^* is the value at which (2.3) would be satisfied if $>$ were replaced by an equality. The proportion falls with the extent of leakage (l), with the level of well-being of the recipients (Y_0), and the price of giving. It rises with the level of income of the donor. Where a transfer is made, the amount given depends on these factors and also on m. A rise in m means that donors are extending their range of concern.

The identification model provides in this way a vehicle to analyze the factors influencing the proportion of the population who make charitable gifts for development and the amounts given. More generally, the case study illustrates how detailed consideration of a specific application can lead to a formulation appropriate to that case.

2.3 Lifetime Giving and Charitable Bequests

The model of giving described in the previous section is a static model, but charitable giving is part of a dynamic lifetime process. Adapting the standard life-cycle model, with a known lifetime T and no uncertainty, the utility from charitable giving is given by (as in Watson, 1984):

$$\int_0^T e^{-\rho t} U(C_t, D_t)\mathrm{d}t + e^{-\rho t}\Phi[A(T) - B, B] \qquad (2.4)$$

The first term gives the discounted (at rate ρ) utility anticipated from the stream of consumption, Ct, and charitable donations, Dt, over the lifetime T; the second term gives the utility produced (in anticipation) by the estate where A(T) of assets are held at death, of which B is a charitable bequest and the remainder passes to the heirs. Of particular interest is the timing of donations and the role of corner conditions. A person may concentrate giving in specific periods or, indeed, postpone all giving until the date of death. Another person may make lifetime gifts to charity but leave all of the estate to the heirs. Or people may give continuously, as for example they tithe a proportion of their income in each period.

The treatment of giving by Watson assumes that the motive is warm-glow. I have, however, argued that for the specific application to giving for overseas development we should adopt an outcome-focused approach, such as the identification model. In that case, we have to consider the implications of timing for the effectiveness of giving. In a steady-state, with equal numbers in each generation, there may be no difference. Such a model may, for example, apply to giving for end-of-life care, which could be financed by donations at any stage of the life-cycle, providing that the pattern is repeated from generation to generation. The situation with overseas development is quite different in that it is based on the assumption that the need for development assistance is a temporary, if long, phase in history. The ambition of development charities is to see their role come to an end. If that is the case, then contributions are much more valuable earlier than later: time is of the essence. The rate of return, it is argued, is higher than that which can be obtained from the savings by the potential donor. Put another way, the cost of achieving target outcomes is rising over time, as wages rise in the recipient countries. There is therefore a high return to carrying out labour-intensive development projects now rather than several decades later.

Such considerations need to be incorporated into the model of charitable giving. We need however to go further and to consider the challenge that has been raised to the underlying approach to intertemporal decision-making, a challenge that has been well summarized by Thaler and Benartzi: "it is rare to find someone who has spent much time determining the optimal savings rate, given all the uncertainties about future rates of return, income flows, retirement plans, health, and so forth. Instead, most people attempt to cope with complexity by adopting simple heuristics, or rules of thumb, to aid decision-making" (2007, Executive Summary). In a sense, the complexity is now transferred to the explanation of behavior. A wide range of considerations is introduced. Following the classification by Knoll (2010), there are issues concerning—in addition to the use of heuristics—information, the nature of intertemporal choice, and the decision context. Informational issues include those concerned with the future opportunity cost of giving (the future needs of the individual), future income streams, future tax and other policies, and those concerned with the outcomes from giving for development. Where people exhibit ambiguity aversion, they may decide not to contribute on the grounds that there are conflicting views about the effectiveness of development assistance, and in the absence of convincing evidence they may rely on anecdotal reports. The degree of self-control implied by the maximization of the lifetime utility function (4) has been questioned, with alternative models of hyperbolic discounting, of procrastination, or of limited attention. Donors may rationally restrict the range of information that they consider, as argued in the case of tax relief for charitable donations in the UK by Scharf and Smith (2010). The role of social context in influencing giving has been demonstrated in field experiments, such as that by DellaVigna, List, and Malmendier (2012) concerning door-to-door solicitation.

These considerations open up new avenues. In deciding which to pursue, it is necessary to consider the specific case in hand and to impose the structure appropriate to that application. In the case of charitable giving for development, there are certain elements in what I have already discussed. The identification approach may be seen as a specific form of "framing," where the visualization of the problem reduces it to a manageable form. Tithes are an example of a heuristic, re-inforced by religious or social pressure. We can however go further, as is illustrated here by the UK study by Atkinson, Backus, and Micklewright (2009) of the multiple stages involved in determining charitable bequests for development.

The determinants of charitable bequests, and particularly the impact of estate taxation, has been the subject of a number of studies, those in the US including Boskin (1976), Feldstein (1976) and Bakija, Gale, and Slemrod (2003). This literature has tended, however, to collapse the decision to leave a charitable bequest into a single stage, whereas it is fruitful to consider separately the different stages in the decision process. Breaking down the process in this way allows more structure to be placed. The first stage concerns the decision to leave significant assets at death. The second stage concerns the disposition of these assets. This depends on the freedom of bequest, which varies considerably across countries, and even within countries. In the UK, there is broadly freedom of bequest in England and Wales (although legislation can impede this freedom *ex post* and threaten charitable bequests if the deceased is deemed to have unreasonably failed to make sufficient provision for his or her family, see Hannah and McGregor-Lowndes, 2008). In contrast, under Scots law a testator is not free to distribute his or her estate in an unrestricted manner. In other countries, testamentary freedom is limited where there are legal systems that embody the Napoleonic Code. In France, for example, there is a reserved portion for children and other heirs, and this cannot be over-ridden by a will. In such cases, there is less incentive to make a will, but it is surprising that in countries where there is freedom of bequest a sizeable minority of wealth-holders fail to do so. In the UK study (Atkinson, Backus, and Micklewright, 2009) of some 240,000 estates in 2007–8, there were 15% who left significant wealth but died intestate. The proportion making a will rose with wealth but, remarkably, some people died leaving estates of over £1 million without making a will.

The third stage is that of including, or not including, a charitable bequest. The UK study found that 16% of testate estates did so. In view of the difference in testamentary freedom between Scotland, one hand, and England and Wales, on the other, it is interesting to see the difference:

	England and Wales	Scotland
% testate	84.9	81.7
% of testate leaving charitable bequests	16.8	11.2
Combined effect	14.3	9.2

The differences are not large but are in the direction expected given the greater restrictions in Scotland on the disposal of the estate. The UK overall rate of 16% making charitable bequests, combined with a testacy rate of 85%, and the fact that significant wealth was left in only some 43% of all deaths, implies that in 6% of deaths in Britain in 2007–8 the will contained a charitable bequest. There is however a fourth stage: a testamentary bequest may be conditional. For example, a bequest may be conditional on there being no surviving spouse, or on the children having reached the age of majority. In the UK study, absolute (i.e. unconditional) bequests were made in 73% of cases. It should be noted that this hurdle is missed by studies based purely on estate tax returns. Bequests that are conditional do not appear in these data where the conditions are not met; and no distinction can be drawn between absolute bequests and those bequests that were conditional and the conditions were satisfied. Although the estate data measure correctly the amount of wealth transferred to charities (for estates above the tax threshold), they may be seen as understating the full extent of the charitable intent of the decedents concerned.

Breaking down the bequest process in this way shows that there are at least four hurdles that have to be jumped before a charity finally benefits from a bequest. Considering these stages separately provides a structure for seeking to understand the determinants, including the role of public policy, which may operate to differing degrees at different stages.

2.4 The Welfare Economics of Giving

In considering public policy we have both positive questions as to how policy impacts on charitable giving and normative questions as to how public policy should be determined. In the case of giving for overseas development, the latter include the general question of tax relief for charities and the specific question as to how far ODA should take account of individual action. The answers to such normative questions depend on the form of social objectives, which—since the demise of the study of welfare economics—have not been the subject of sufficient critical attention by economists. The topic of this chapter does in fact raise two important challenges to welfare economics.

The first challenge concerns the treatment of individual motives for charitable giving. It has been argued that these should be ignored when formulating the social objectives. In his discussion of warm-glow preferences for giving for public goods, Diamond argues that "the fact that warm glows improve the description of individual behavior does not necessarily imply that social welfare should be defined including warm glows" (2006, p. 915). The D term in the utility function should be ignored when forming a social welfare function based on individual well-being. Here I have suggested that giving for development should be modeled in terms of outcomes, not warm-glow, but objections can also be leveled in this case. With the additive formulation (2), the donor's utility consists of an element arising from the person's privately oriented preferences and an element reflecting the person's concern for others. "Concern" implies that the well-being of others enters positively or at least non-negatively ($\delta \geq 0$). If the sign of δ were to be reversed, most people would agree that such feelings should be disregarded. Envy or jealousy has no place in the social welfare function. What about the positive feelings that we have been considering? Should these also be disregarded? The main argument that has been advanced is that of double-counting. Hammond (1987) argues that, by taking (2) for the donor, and $U(C)$ for the recipient, the privately-oriented preferences for the recipient are being given a weight of $(1 + \delta)$, whereas the donor has only a weight of 1. Here, however, the specific context means that we can reject this argument, since the recipients are in a different country. There would only be double-counting if we were to sum over the entire world population.

This brings us to the second challenge posed by the case of giving for overseas development. Whose well-being should enter the social welfare function? It could be all world citizens—a cosmopolitan social welfare function, but most governments act as though they are concerned only with their citizens. The UK Government Green Book "Appraisal and evaluation" states explicitly that "generally, proposals should not proceed if, despite a net benefit overall, there is a net cost to the UK" (HM Treasury 2013, p. 21n). At the same time, it would be hard to justify ODA on this basis, so that the government appears to be speaking with more than one voice.

Neither cosmopolitanism nor pure nationalism seems to be justified. What intermediate path can we follow? Suppose that the social welfare function is restricted to citizens, but takes account of their extended sympathy. In its simplest form, the social welfare function is then the sum of the individual functions (2), where the well-being of overseas recipients enters with a weight δ, and the concern of a rich nation is with m times the number of its own citizens. Alternatively, we could argue directly in terms of the social welfare function that the counterpart at the level of the nation to the identification approach is that each donor country takes a proportionate share of responsibility for the funding of development. Since the total population of Development Assistance Committee countries is approximately equal to the number of people below the MDG poverty line, m = 1 would provide a natural starting point. Differing degrees of concern with world poverty would then be captured by differences in δ.

2.5 Conclusions

In this chapter, I have described some of the issues that arise in studying charitable giving for development in the UK. This has been a specific project, but I have argued that there are lessons more widely for the economics of charitable giving, and indeed for economics. There are three main conclusions. The first is that we can only make progress by putting more structure on the model of decision-making. The imposition of structure is particularly important—for the economics of charitable giving and for microeconomics in general—as we increasingly come to challenge textbook theory. The exploration of the multi-stage bequest process is an example of an attempt to provide a framework within which different factors can be identified. The second conclusion is that the form adopted has, as in this example, to be tailored to the specific application. It was the specific features of giving for development that led to the identification approach; other forms of giving may be appropriately treated in other ways. Generality is always prized in economics, but this may come at the cost of limiting what we can say. It would be quite reasonable for utility-maximization to remain the cornerstone of consumer demand analysis but for other models to be applied to long-term inter-temporal decisions. The third conclusion is that we need to reconsider the underlying welfare economics, and specifically how we formulate national welfare criteria in a global context. This conclusion too is of wider applicability and touches all policy design issues that cross national borders.

References

Andreoni, James (2006). "Chapter 18 Philanthropy," in Serge-Christophe Kolm and Jean Mercier Ythier, eds, *Handbook of the Economics of Giving, Altruism and Reciprocity*, Vol. 2 (Amsterdam: Elsevier), pp. 1201–1269.

Atkinson, A. B., (2009). "Giving Overseas and Public Policy," *Journal of Public Economics, 93* (5–6), 647–653.

Atkinson, A. B., P. G. Backus, and J. Micklewright, (2009). "Charitable Bequests and Wealth at Death in Great Britain," <http://eprints.soton.ac.uk/65909> March.

Atkinson, Anthony B., Peter G. Backus, John Micklewright, Cathy Pharoah, and Sylke V. Schnepf, (2012). "Charitable Giving for Overseas Development: UK Trends over a Quarter Century," *Journal of the Royal Statistical Society: Series A (Statistics in Society), 175* (1), 167–190.

Atkinson, Richard and Amy Eastwood, (2007). "Public Attitudes to Overseas Giving: Does Government Make a Difference?," <http://eprints.soton.ac.uk/48324> September.

Bakija, Jon M, William G. Gale, and Joel B. Slemrod, (2003). "Charitable Bequests and Taxes on Inheritance and Estates: Aggregate Evidence from Across States and Time," *American Economic Review, 93* (2), 366–370.

Boskin, Michael J., (1976). "Estate Taxation and Charitable Bequests," *Journal of Public Economics, 5* (1–2), 27–56.

Charities Aid Foundation (2006). *Charity Trends 2005*. West Mailing CAF.

DellaVigna, Stefano, (2009). "Psychology and Economics: Evidence from the Field," *Journal of Economic Literature, 47* (2), 315–372.

DellaVigna, Stefano, John A. List, and Ulrike Malmendier, (2012). "Testing for Altruism and Social Pressure in Charitable Giving," *The Quarterly Journal of Economics, 127* (1), 1–56.

Diamond, Peter, (2006). "Optimal Tax Treatment of Private Contributions for Public Goods with and without Warm Glow Preferences," *Journal of Public Economics, 90* (4–5), 897–919.

Edgeworth, Francis Ysidro, (1881). *Mathematical Psychics: An Essay on the Application of Mathematics to the Moral Sciences.* (New York: C. Kegan Paul & Company).

Feldstein, Martin, (1976). "Charitable Bequests, Estate Taxation, and Intergenerational Wealth Transfers," in R. E. Grieson, ed., *Research Papers, sponsored by the Commission on Private Philanthropy and Public Needs* (Lexington: Lexington Books).

Hammond, Peter J., (1987). "Altruism," in Steven N. Durlauf and Lawrence E. Blume, eds, *The New Palgrave Dictionary of Economics*, 2 ed. (Basingstoke: Nature Publishing Group), p. 1.

Hannah, Frances M. and Myles McGregor-Lowndes, (2008). "From Testamentary Freedom to Testamentary Duty: Finding the Balance," <http://eprints.qut.edu.au/15464/>.

Jones, Andrew M. and John W. Posnett, (1993). "The Economics of Charity," in N. Barr and D. Whynes, eds, *Current Issues in the Economics of Welfare* (New York: St. Martin's Press), pp. 130–152.

Knoll, Melissa, (2010). "The Role of Behavioral Economics and Behavioral Decision Making in Americans' Retirement Savings Decisions," SSRN Scholarly Paper ID 1702815, Social Science Research Network (Rochester, NY).

Kolm, Serge-Christophe and Jean Mercier Ythier, (2006). *Handbook of the Economics of Giving, Altruism and Reciprocity*, Volume 2: *Applications* (Amsterdam: Elsevier).

Scharf, Kimberley A. and Sarah Smith, (2010). "Rational Inattention to Subsidies for Charitable Contributions," CEPR Discussion Paper 7760.

Sen, Amartya K., (1966). "Labour Allocation in a Cooperative Enterprise," *Review of Economic Studies, 33* (4), 361.

Sugden, Robert, (1982). "On the Economics of Philanthropy," *Economic Journal, 92* (366), 341–50.

Thaler, Richard H. and Shlomo Benartzi, (2007). "The Behavioral Economics of Retirement Savings Behavior," AARP. Washington DC.

Treasury, HM, (2013). "Green Book," London: HM Treasury.

Watson, Harry, (1984). "A Note on the Effects of Taxation on Charitable Giving Over the Life Cycle and Beyond," *Quarterly Journal of Economics, 99* (3), 639.

3

Charitable Giving and Tax Policy in the US

Charles T. Clotfelter

In several important ways, US tax policy favors charitable giving and nonprofit organizations. Not only are nonprofit organizations generally exempted from income and property taxes, but most contributions to them from living donors, corporations, and estates are also tax-deductible. This favorable tax treatment is one important component of a more general American approach to the provision of public goods. The nation's tax policy toward charitable giving has had three broad effects. First, this tax policy allows many citizens to gain a sense of participation that they might not otherwise have, by choosing the causes and organizations that will receive their donations. Institutionally, this sense of participation is reflected and enhanced by a very prominent nonprofit sector. Second, this policy has the effect of handing over to wealthy individuals an extraordinary amount of influence over the allocation of public funds. As a result of these two effects, American tax policy contains an inherent tension between participatory citizenship and elitism. Third, because it operates through a tax deduction, tax policy toward charitable giving is vulnerable to inadvertent modification simply as a result of otherwise unrelated tinkering with the income tax.

The chapter begins in Section 3.1 by providing some broader context for understanding the role of tax policy toward charitable giving. Section 3.2 describes the basic components of American tax policy, its implications for incentives for donors, and some of the prominent tax policy issues that arise in connection with the charitable deduction. Section 3.3 discusses the unusually large role played by wealthy donors by virtue of the charitable deduction. Section 3.4 examines the possible effect of tax reform on charitable giving. The Conclusion offers a brief recapitulation.

3.1 American Exceptionalism, the Social Contract, and Charitable Giving

Compared with other advanced countries, the United States has developed a distinctive approach to meeting social needs. It relies less on direct government provision and compulsory taxation and more on voluntary provision. In 2007 government social spending was 16.2% of GDP in the US, compared with 19.2% in the Organisation for Economic Co-operation and Development (OECD), as shown in table 3.1. The corresponding ratios in Continental Europe's largest economies, France and Germany, were 28.4% and 25.2%, respectively. As has been frequently documented, the consequences of the comparatively weak American social safety net are higher poverty rates and greater income inequality, after taxes and transfers. For example, Smeeding (2006, Table 4) calculates that government spending on social insurance and social assistance reduced the poverty rate in the US by 26%, compared with an average of 61% in the OECD as a whole.[1] Similarly, the United States generally lags behind Europe in public expenditures for

Table 3.1 Public and Private Social Expenditures as Percent of GDP, Selected Countries, 2007

Country	Public	Private	Total
Australia	16.0	3.8	19.8
Canada	16.9	5.3	22.2
France	28.4	2.9	31.3
Germany	25.2	2.9	28.1
Netherlands	20.1	6.9	27.0
United Kingdom	20.5	5.8	26.3
OECD Total	19.2	2.5	21.17
USA	**16.2**	**10.5**	**26.7**

Note: Social expenditures include cash benefits, direct and indirect in-kind provision of goods and services, and tax breaks with social purposes. These must entail redistribution or compulsory participation. Tax expenditures for charitable contributions are counted as private, since their disposition is controlled by individuals, not government.

Source: OECD Factbook 2011, "Economic, Environmental and Social Statistics, Public and Private Expenditures, <http://dx.doi.org/10.1787/888893250710 3>.

[1] See also Neubourg et al. (2007, p. 7) for an analysis with similar findings. Comparisons use poverty rates defined relative to each country's median income.

health, education, and culture.[2] Alesina, Glaeser, and Sacerdote (2001, pp. 46, 55, and 57) offer several explanations for this difference, including racial heterogeneity, Protestantism, and an American tendency to ascribe poverty to laziness.

In contrast to its stingy public provision, however, the United States tends to be a leader when it comes to private provision, expenditures controlled by individuals rather than the government, some of which is subsidized by the government through tax breaks. As shown in table 3.1, the portion of GDP the US devoted to social expenditures not controlled by government was 10.5% in 2007, well above the OECD average of 2.5%. Part of this private expenditure comes in the form of tax expenditures, tax revenue that is sacrificed as a result of exemptions, deductions, or other exclusion from taxation, such as the exclusion for health premiums, pension contributions, and the deduction for charitable contributions. As such, these OECD-defined "private" expenditures are actually funded, in part, by the US government.[3] Because tax expenditures for social purposes have an effect similar to direct government provision, one author (Howard, 1997) has referred to them as the "hidden welfare state."

A centerpiece of this shadow welfare state is charitable giving. According to household surveys, Americans contribute about 1.7% of national income, a far higher percentage than in other developed countries, as shown in table 3.2. When combined with contributions by corporations and charitable bequests from estates, Americans give roughly 2% of their income to nonprofit organizations, a ratio that has held rather steady for decades.[4] Scholars have made a great deal of this tradition of personal generosity, giving it a prominent place in the larger portrait of America's distinctive approach in addressing social needs. Indeed, the American record of giving and volunteering has been celebrated as often as its weak government safety net has been decried. From this laudatory perspective, the generosity of spirit

[2] See OECD Factbook 2011, <http://www.oecd-ilibrary.org/economics/oecd-factbook_18147364>, (3/20/12).

[3] The OECD defines "social expenditures" as follows: "Social expenditure comprises cash benefits, direct in-kind provision of goods and services, and tax breaks with social purposes. Benefits may be targeted at low-income households, the elderly, disabled, sick, unemployed, or young persons. To be considered social, programmes have to involve either redistribution of resources across households or compulsory participation. Social benefits are classified as public when general government (that is central, state, and local governments, including social security funds) controls the relevant financial flows. All social benefits not provided by general government are considered private. Private transfers between households are not considered as social." For an official run-down of US tax expenditures, see US Office of Management and Budget (2010), chapter 17, "Tax Expenditures."

[4] Wing et al. (2008, Figure 3.1, p. 73). For a summary of aggregate giving from these various sources over time, see the annual publication *Giving USA*.

Table 3.2 National Giving as Percent of GDP, Selected Countries

Country	Percent
Australia	0.69
Canada	0.72
France	0.14
Germany	0.22
Netherlands	0.45
United Kingdom	0.73
USA	**1.67**

Note: Based on surveys of adults covering various years between 2000 and 2004.

Source: *International Comparisons of Charitable Giving* (Kent, UK: Charities Aid Foundation, November 2006, p.6).

revealed by the country's high rate of charitable giving is inextricably wedded to the country's historical reliance on non-governmental organizations to address social problems and provide collective goods. Political scientist Lester Salamon sees in this model a tension between "two seemingly contradictory principles" honored by Americans: individualism and solidarity.[5] No history of the American nonprofit sector can be complete without a quotation taken from the eloquent Frenchman Alexis de Tocqueville, who was enamored by much of what he encountered in his visit to the United States in 1831. He may be best known for his description of the American tendency to form voluntary associations: "In no country in the world has the principle of association been more successfully used or applied to a greater multitude of objects than in America."[6] This theme has been embraced by many American historians of the nonprofit sector, and highlighting this distinguishing national characteristic often goes hand in hand with noting with approval the tradition of voluntary giving that supports it. For example, Bremner writes: "We do not need to exaggerate the extent of our national generosity to recognize that voluntary benevolence has played a large role and performed important functions in American society."[7]

There is no shortage of evidence to illustrate the significance of the nonprofit sector in the United States. In no other developed country are there, for example, so many thriving and prominent nonprofit universities. Of the 15 American universities listed among the *Times*

[5] Salamon (2002, p. 10).
[6] Quoted from *Democracy in America* in Hammack (1998, p. 143).
[7] Bremner (1977, p. 89).

of London's top 20 in the world, 12 are private.[8] Nonprofit institutions are similarly prominent among the country's leading medical centers, museums, and symphony orchestras. Religious organizations, most of them small congregations, are ubiquitous. Many social services are provided by religious and other nonprofit organizations, and "community chest" funds provide a significant portion of spending for public needs, as indicated by the figures given above. Nonprofit organizations employ nearly a tenth of the American workforce.[9]

One inevitable consequence of this reliance on independent organizations is decentralization of power. Letting a thousand flowers bloom fits nicely, in terms of political philosophy, with America's pluralistic principles. According to Prewitt (2006, pp. 39–41), these principles are aligned with the country's historical preferences for weak and unobtrusive government. The significance of all this for the current chapter is in the revenue side of this sector. By leaving such a large share of the funding up to individuals, the system takes much of the decision-making away from legislatures and hands it over to individual donors. For a country that historically has revered individual liberty, this devolution of responsibility is attractive and natural. In allowing a deduction for charitable donations, American tax law in effect recognizes that donations replace government spending and, by extension, gives legitimacy to the social value of donors' preferences. Not only is this decentralization of decision making consistent with pluralism, but some observers also see it as a market-like mechanism that makes public provision more efficient, a viewpoint concisely stated by Yale law professor Stephen Carter:

> The charitable deduction also helps resolve an information problem: Government officials, no matter how well-intentioned, cannot know all the places where donations are needed, or the form that will be most useful. The deduction is democracy in action. By encouraging individuals to make their own choices on how to spend money for the public good, the deduction makes society as a whole better off.[10]

Despite the frequently obvious disadvantages of inadequate resources and duplicated effort, such a system also offers the advantage of

[8] Website for the *Times* of London, <http://www.timeshighereducation.co.uk/world-university-rankings/2010-2011/top-200.html> (3/17/12).

[9] Wing et al. (2008, Table 1.8, p. 20) estimate that nonprofits employed 9.7% of the US workforce in 2005.

[10] Stephen L. Carter, "Ending Charity Tax Break Will Hurt Poor Most," *Bloomberg*, November 22, 2011; <http://www.bloomberg.com/news/print/2011-11-23/ending-charity-tax-break-would-hurt-poor-commentary-by-stephen-l-carter.html> (3/8/12).

efficiency-enhancing competition, such as that which occurs among research universities.[11]

By almost any yardstick, the magnitude of charitable giving in the US is large. For the year 2010, donations from living individuals amounted to some $211.8 billion. Corporations contributed an additional $15.3 billion, and decedents left another $22.8 billion in charitable bequests.[12] For individuals in the United States, making donations to tax exempt organizations is quite common, with more than two-thirds of all households reporting making such donations. Both average contributions and the percentage of households who report any contributions tend to rise with age into middle age and then go back down.[13] The pattern of average giving is much smoother when households are arranged by income, and the percentage that make contributions also tends to rise with income. As a percentage of annual income, deductible contributions make a U-shape pattern, falling with income up to the $200,000 to $500,000 category, after which they rise again.[14] As shown in figure 3.1 however, the taxpayers responsible for the rising portion at high incomes account for a relatively small share of total contributions. Differences across individuals have also been noted between those who attend church and those who do not, with the former group more likely to give. Other variables that have been found in past studies to be positively related to giving include education, marriage, number of children, home ownership, living in a city under one million in population, and having parents who gave regularly.[15]

One fact of great significance for any discussion of US tax policy toward charitable giving is that donative preferences differ markedly

[11] For an argument to this effect, see Clotfelter (2010, Introduction).

[12] *Giving USA 2010* news release, June 20, 2011; <http://www.aafrc.org/press_releases/gusa/GUSA-2011-Final-Release.pdf> (3/18/12).

[13] See Clotfelter (1997).

[14] Note that this U-shape pattern is partly due to the fact that tax return data in the US only provides information on the charitable donations of people who choose to itemize their deductions, which introduces a bias in the estimates of overall donations. The reason is that the decision to itemize is endogenously related to the size of one's charitable donation. People with unusually large charitable donations are more likely to itemize than people with similar characteristics but with smaller itemized deductions, because the former group is more likely to have itemized deductions that exceed the standard deduction. The extent to which this biases estimates of mean charitable donations by income class and year varies greatly by income class and by year. The bias is much more extreme at lower income levels, because people with lower incomes are far less likely than higher income people to have non-charitable itemized deductions large enough to exceed the standard deduction, and those that do not tend to have non-charitable itemized deductions tend to be further below the standard deduction threshold. Thus, for low- and middle-income people, data on charitable donations from US tax return data is really only representative of people who are at the extreme right-end tail of the generosity distribution.

[15] See Clotfelter (1997).

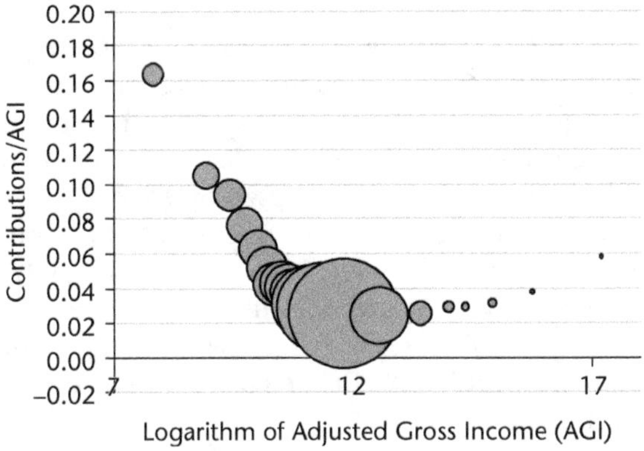

Figure 3.1 Contributions as Percent of Income

Notes: Size of points are proportional to contributions. Note also that tax return data in the US only provides information on the charitable donations of people who choose to itemize their deductions, which introduces a bias in the estimates of overall donations. The reason is that the decision to itemize is endogenously related to the size of one's charitable donation. People with unusually large charitable donations are more likely to itemize than people with similar characteristics but with smaller itemized deductions, because the former group is more likely to have itemized deductions that exceed the standard deduction. The extent to which this biases estimates of mean charitable donations by income class and year varies greatly by income class and by year. The bias is much more extreme at lower income levels, because people with lower incomes are far less likely than higher income people to have non-charitable itemized deductions large enough to exceed the standard deduction, and those that do not tend to have non-charitable itemized deductions tend to be further below the standard deduction threshold. Thus, for low- and middle-income people, data on charitable donations from US tax return data is really only representative of people who are at the extreme right-end tail of the generosity distribution.

Sources: IRS, Statistics of Income 2009, Table 2.1.

across individuals. That preferences differ from one person to the next is not surprising, and indeed the efficiency of the tax deduction that Carter notes above depends crucially on the ability of each individual taxpayer to direct a portion of the national tax subsidy to the charity of his or her choice. One taxpayer donates to the local soup kitchen while another chooses to support medical research. But there is one dimension of systematic variation in the types of organizations supported that is worthy of special note. On average, the types of organizations favored by donors differ systematically up and down the income distribution. For individuals of modest means, religious organizations are far and away the most favored type of donee. As shown in table 3.3, contributions to religious organizations (even subtracting the portion that are ultimately used to provide aid to the needy outside of congregations) made up two-thirds of the contributions made by individuals with incomes under $100,000 in 2005. For those in the next highest income class, $100,000 to $200,000, giving to religious organizations remained the leading category, though its share was only a little more than half. For the two highest income categories ($200,000 to $1 million and $1 million or more), religion was eclipsed by education, which turns out to be mainly higher education. Owing mainly to these preference patterns and the sheer magnitude of donations made by high-income individuals, donations to educational institutions are almost half as large as the total giving directed to religious institutions. And the totals given to education, health, and the arts depend almost exclusively on gifts from the affluent.

In light of America's heavy reliance on private, as opposed to public, social expenditures, it is natural to wonder how much redistribution is actually accomplished by way of contributions. As noted at the beginning of this section, the public sector in the US, through taxes and transfers, brings about considerably less poverty reduction than is the norm in Europe. That charitable contributions in the US bring about at least some redistribution to the poor is suggested by the information given in table 3.3 on the distribution of contributions. In addition to the 7.5% devoted to basic needs, certainly a portion of contributions to health, education, and other organizations would also be considered redistributive. Still, much of it is not. These patterns of giving by income class have particular policy relevance because not all contributions receive the same tax treatment, a subject to which I now turn.

Table 3.3 Contribution by Income and Subsector, 2005, as Percent of Total

Subsector	Income				
	Less than $100,000	$100,000 to $200,000	$200,000 to $1 million	$1 million or more	Total
Religion	23.7	4.5	8.3	3.4	40.0
Combined	3.0	0.9	4.0	0.8	8.8
Basic needs (1)	3.7	1.0	2.1	0.8	7.5
Health	1.2	0.4	1.9	5.1	8.7
Education	1.1	0.5	11.5	5.1	18.2
Arts	0.4	0.2	5.4	3.1	9.1
Other	2.4	0.5	2.9	1.9	7.8
Total	35.6	7.9	36.2	20.3	100.0

Note: (1) Providing food, shelter, or other necessities.

Source: Patterns of Household Charitable Giving by Income Group, 2005 (Indianapolis Center on Philanthropy, Summer 2007), Table 9.

3.2 The Basics of the US Income Tax Policy

The centerpiece of US tax policy towards charitable giving is the deduction available in the personal income tax, the corporation income tax, and the estate and gift tax.[16] The modern US individual income tax was passed in 1913. The deduction for donations to nonprofit charitable and educational organizations was added in 1917, a year in which Congress increased tax rates to finance the war effort, raising the top marginal tax rate from 15% to 67%. Arguing for the deduction was Senator Henry Hollis of New Hampshire, who stated, "we impose these very heavy taxes on incomes, [and] that will be the first place where these very wealthy men will be tempted to economize, namely, in donations to charity."[17] Very wealthy men, indeed: to qualify for the top tax rate, a taxpayer needed an income of $35 million in 2011 dollars. Those with incomes of a mere $1 million were subject only to a 16% marginal rate. Top marginal rates fluctuated thereafter, falling as low as 24% (in 1929) and rising as high as 94% (1944–5).[18] In 1944, the Congress introduced a standard deduction, after which most taxpayers stopped itemizing deductions. In 1945 only 17% of taxpayers itemized, a percentage that crept up over time to a peak of 48% in 1970, after which the minimum standard deduction amount was increased and, eventually, indexed to inflation.[19] Except for a brief period in the 1980s, nonitemizers received no tax deduction for making charitable donations.[20] Finally, the deduction for contributions is limited in any year to no more than half of a taxpayer's income, with the excess being carried forward as many as five more years.[21]

[16] Contributions are deductible if given to nonprofit organizations described in section 501(c)3, defined as "charitable, religious, educational, scientific, literary, fostering national or international amateur sports competition, and preventing cruelty to children or animals." A deduction is not allowed for one group of 501(c)3 organizations, namely, those testing for public safety. See IRS, <http://www.irs.gov/charities/charitable/article/0,,id=175418,00.html> (3/26/12).

[17] *Congressional Record*, September 7, 1917, p. 6728, as quoted in Clotfelter (1985, p. 31), which mistakenly reports that the top marginal rate in 1917 was 15%.

[18] Tax Foundation, *Federal Individual Income Tax Rates History*, <http://www.taxfoundation.org/files/fed_individual_rate_history_nominal&adjusted-20110909.pdf> (3/8/12).

[19] Clotfelter (1985, pp. 25–6).

[20] As stipulated in the Economic Recovery Tax Act of 1981, nonitemizers could deduct 25% of the first $100 (married filing jointly) of donations in 1982 and 1983, 25% of the first $300 in 1984, 50% of all contributions in 1985, and 100% of all contributions in 1986, after which the provision went away (Ackerman and Auten 2006, p. 510).

[21] The rules are summarized in IRS, Charitable Contribution Deductions, <http://www.irs.gov/charities/charitable/article/0,,id=134331,00.html> (4/26/12). Contributions to most private foundations and a few other types of charitable organizations are limited to 30% of adjusted gross income and gifts to some organizations are limited to 20%. See IRS, Exempt Organizations Select Check, <http://www.irs.gov/charities/article/0,,id=252661,00.html>

It follows from these few details of tax structure that two facts above all determine how any given taxpayer's contributions will be treated: itemization status and marginal tax rate. As a practical matter, almost anybody who spends a sufficient amount on a handful of items will usually find it advantageous to be an itemizer. Since two of the most important of these items for middle-income taxpayers are mortgage interest and property taxes, itemization for the middle class is more or less coincident with home ownership.[22] The effect of becoming an itemizer is to lower the net-of-tax cost of making contributions, defined as the amount of net income or potential consumption that is forfeited when a dollar is given away as a charitable contribution. For anyone who is an itemizer, this net cost, or "tax price" (p), of giving away cash is defined simply, $p = 1 - m$, where m is the marginal tax rate on income. For a taxpayer facing a marginal tax rate of 35% and who itemizes deductions, for example, giving one more dollar in contributions, because it reduces taxable income by $1 and tax by 35 cents, ends up costing the taxpayer only 65 cents. So the tax price is said to be 0.65. Reflecting the variation in top marginal tax rates over time, figure 3.2 shows how the tax price of giving cash for top-bracket taxpayers has varied over the last 50 years. In 1960, the tax price of making cash gifts for the most affluent taxpayers was a mere 9 cents per dollar of giving, owing to the 91% top marginal tax rate existing at the time. Over the next five decades, the tax price of giving generally rose, as Congress periodically cut the top marginal tax rate, first to 70%, then to 50% in the 1981 tax act, and again following the 1986 tax reform act to 28%. As of 2011, the top marginal tax rate was 35%, making the tax price of giving cash 0.65.

Other provisions of the income tax, especially those applying primarily to wealthy taxpayers, complicate this simple relationship. The most important such complication relates to gifts of appreciated property. When an appreciated asset is sold, at least a portion of any capital gains is subject to taxation, unless the asset is contributed.[23] Therefore,

(4/26/12). There has been and will be a further percentage reduction on all itemized deductions for taxpayers whose AGI exceeds a specific threshold, with total itemized deductions being reduced by as much as 20% (Ackerman and Auten 2006, p. 512; CBO 2011a, p. 2).

[22] Some have pointed to the connection between these two deductions as one of the absurdities of the tax: owning a house has become virtually a necessary and sufficient condition for receiving a government subsidy for donations. See, for example, Richard H. Thaler, "Its Time to Rethink the Charity Deduction," *New York Times*, December 18, 2010.

[23] There are notable exceptions to this exception. For contributed non-stock assets that cannot be used by the receiving organization for its exempt purpose, only the basis is deductible. Gifts of appreciated property made to private foundations are also limited to the

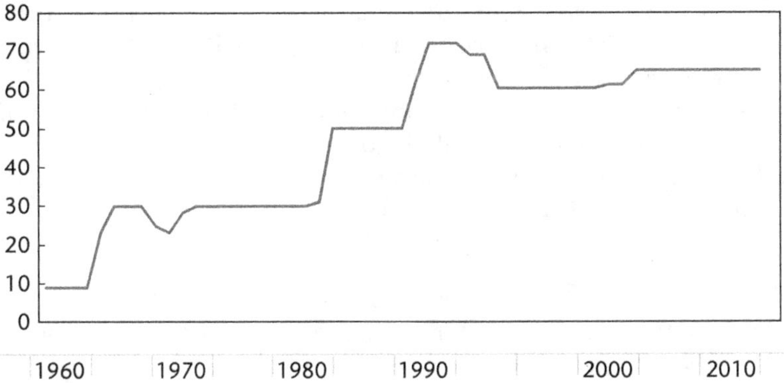

Figure 3.2 Price of Giving Cash at Top Marginal Tax Rate, 1960–2012
Notes: Price calculated as 100 minus the top marginal tax rate on taxable income.

making a contribution using appreciated property can lower a taxpayer's tax price even more than donating cash.[24]

A second, and related, complication is the Alternative Minimum Tax (AMT), a tax provision which is in effect a parallel income tax. Whether it or the regular tax applies to any particular taxpayer in a given year will determine the tax price of giving, but this is not something that is always easy to predict in advance of the ultimate calculation of one's taxes, a predicament that can call for very sophisticated tax planning surrounding gifts.[25] As a matter of policy, the elements of the AMT tax base may have an especially big effect on the price of giving appreciated property. In 1986 Congress made the portion of a gift of property that was appreciation a "tax preference item" in the Alternative Minimum Tax, which had the effect for taxpayers affected by the AMT of limiting the deduction value for a gift of appreciated property to the basis. For some potential gifts, this provision had the effect of virtually wiping out the bulk of the deduction, particularly of artwork. Museums, in

tax basis, and short-term capital gains are not ignored as long-term gains are (Ackerman and Auten 2006, p. 512). For a description of the limitations on gifts of appreciate property, see IRS, Publication 526, Charitable Contributions, <http://www.irs.gov/pub/irs-pdf/p526.pdf> (4/26/12). See also (Auten, Clotfelter, and Schmalbeck 2000, p. 395).

[24] The actual tax price depends on the tax rate on capital gains income, the portion of the asset value that is appreciated property, and what would have been done with the asset were it not contributed. In formal terms, the tax price of giving away an asset that would otherwise have been sold is p = (1 m (a)(mc)), where a is the portion of the assets value that is appreciation and mc is the marginal tax rate on capital gains income.

[25] See, for example, the tax planning advice offered in Tara Siegel Bernard, "Minimizing A.M.T. Through Charitable Donations," *New York Times*, December 22, 2010.

particular, worried about the potential detrimental effect, and their fears seemed to be confirmed by a drop in gifts right after the rule was introduced. These institutions lobbied, successfully, to have this provision rescinded. Today, museums remain vigilant to the threat of tax reform that would end the ability of taxpayers to donate artwork at market value.[26] In a statement suggesting how important the current treatment is to museums, the Association of Art Museum Directors wrote this for a Senate hearing in 2011:

> The tax treatment of gifts of art has been altered several times since 1969, and donors' behavior has responded directly, immediately and always negatively... [W]e suggest that discouraging gifts to the arts by reducing their tax deductibility would have a counter-productive effect. It would lessen institutions' growing ability to serve the very populations whom Members of Congress most wish charities to serve... The social safety net has many strands; weakening any single strand only diminishes the safety net's overall integrity. Supporting the needy and supporting the arts are not mutually exclusive enterprises.[27]

The attention to the tax price of giving in the preceding paragraphs can be justified on the basis of its presumed behavioral effect. For over three decades, there has been sustained attention and vigorous debate in the public finance literature about the degree to which donors respond to the tax price. Virtually all scholars who have weighed in on the issue conclude that the tax price affects the amount that people donate, and many observers believe that this price effect can be stated in terms of a price elasticity in the range −0.5 to −1.0. An elasticity of −0.5 implies that a 10% decline in the tax price, say from 0.50 to 0.45, would lead to a 5% increase in contributions; an elasticity of −1.0 would imply a 10% increase.[28] Statistical studies also suggest that taxation has an

[26] Auten, Clotfelter, and Schmalbeck (2000, pp. 395–6).

[27] Association of Art Museum Director, Statement Submitted to the United States Senate Committee on Finance, Hearing on tax Reform Options: Incentives for Charitable Giving, October 18, 2011; <http://www.aamd.org/advocacy/documents/Philanthropy Testimony.pdf> (3/8/12).

[28] Since the mid-1970s, scores of empirical studies reporting estimates of the tax-price elasticity of contributions have been published. To illustrate, Clotfelter (1985) cites more than 25 studies reporting on evidence about this elasticity, Bakija and Heim (2011) cite 13 studies, and Fack and Landais (2011) cite 17. Whereas most of the earlier studies produced estimates larger than one in absolute value, more recent studies have tended to produce smaller elasticities in absolute value. One recently published study (Fack and Landais 2010) produces estimates well below 1.0 in absolute value, while another (Bakija and Heim 2011) yields estimates larger than 1.0 in absolute value.

income effect on giving, by affecting taxpayers' disposable income. An increase in tax liability reduces after-tax income and thus contributions. Regardless of the precise values of the price and income elasticities, it is not hard to see how changes in tax rates and other features of the income tax might influence the level of charitable giving. If marginal tax rates are reduced, for example, as they were for the top brackets in 1981 and 1986, the price of giving to itemizers in the affected tax brackets will rise. Depending on what happens to tax liabilities, the economic model would imply that contributions by these taxpayers would be lower, at least in the long run, than they would have been had the change not occurred. Another clear implication is that eliminating the deduction altogether, as has been suggested in numerous proposals in the past couple of decades, would raise the price of giving for all itemizers, again implying (in the absence of large changes in total taxes) a long-run level of contributions lower than what would have been the case under the existing type of income tax.

One perhaps inevitable consequence of the liberal treatment of charitable contributions in the US is abuse. As with dozens of other areas of the income tax, crafty or unscrupulous taxpayers occasionally endeavor to reduce their tax liabilities by pushing the limits of the law. One perennial area of potential abuse involves questionable valuations of assets that are donated. For the common man, this ploy might take the form of claiming an exaggerated value for old clothes donated to the Salvation Army thrift store. Because valuations of this sort mostly work on the honor system, there is often latitude for a taxpayer to overstate the market value of the donated items, should he or she be so inclined. A recent study found surprisingly large amounts claimed for contributions of non-cash items. For those taxpayers claiming a deduction for used clothing, the average amount deducted in 2004 was more than $1,400. For household items, it was more than $1,300 (Ackerman and Auten 2008, Table 4). Similar abuse has been associated with donating used cars, but much of the abuse associated with that form of giving has been eliminated in recent years.[29] The real potential for mischief lies in

[29] It was possible a decade ago to deduct exaggerated values for vehicles whose true market value were far below the value shown on standard publications, and even then the nonprofit organizations typically received only a portion of that, after fundraising companies specializing in these transactions had taken as much as two-thirds of the value. In 2004, the law was changed, requiring vehicles to be donated to low-income individuals. See Tyler Cabot, "The Tow-Away Tax Break: Why Car Donation Programs Benefit Everyone but the Charities They're Intended to Help," Washington Monthly, June 2002, pp. 39–42 and Arden Dale, 'Tax Breaks for Donating a Car," *Wall Street Journal*, July 25, 2008. Such compliance issues are the reason why the charitable deduction appears on the IRSs "Dirty Dozen Tax Scams for 2012" list; <http://www.irs.gov/newsroom/article/0,,id=254383,00.html> (3/16/12).

donations of assets whose value has risen rather than fallen. Thus one tempting form of abuse is exaggerating the value of donated art work, making such behavior a longstanding concern for policy makers and tax authorities. Another suspicious pattern recently documented is gifts of company stock to family foundations and other charities. A study found that a remarkably large proportion of such gifts were made when the company's stock was at its peak price (Yermack 2009).[30]

3.3 The Outsized Role of the Rich

A signal feature of the American grants economy, noted in Section 3.1, is the considerable influence that individuals have over the allocation of public subsidies. For the affluent, this point deserves to be made in bold face type. A Methodist congregation in Kansas can decide to put a steeple on its church building, and the government will subsidize that steeple, but only to the extent that those parishioners itemize their deductions. If, as is often the case in many religious congregations across the country, most members take the standard deduction, there will be little in the way of tax subsidy for that steeple. Now consider a taxpayer who wishes to make a $50,000 gift to Stanford University. A gift of this size might be made to set up a special fund for library collections or for need-based financial aid. Or, for the athletically inclined, a gift of this amount will allow a donor to travel with the Stanford football team to an away game.[31] If this donation is made in cash, American taxpayers, by virtue of the deduction, in effect subsidize the gift to the tune of $17,500, leaving the donor to bear the remaining $32,500.

Three features of the income tax treatment of contributions are particularly conducive to this outsized influence. One is the standard deduction, which effectively limits itemization to a minority of taxpayers, most of whom have above-average incomes. A second is the upside-down nature of the deduction. Owing to the role of itemization and the progressivity of the tax rate structure of the tax, the affluent face the lowest tax price of giving among all taxpayers. Third, the especially favorable treatment of gifts of appreciated property, which is held disproportionately by the affluent, further reduces the tax price.

[30] In addition, Yermack (2009) also found that stock given to family foundations was held rather than sold, allowing the donor to retain voting power in the corporation.

[31] Stanford's athletic booster organization, the Buck-Cardinal Club, publishes a chart showing the benefits available at various giving levels. A gift of $50,000 enrolls the donor in the Directors Circle and entitles the donor "to travel with the football team to a select away game (maximum of two people)," <http://grfx.cstv.com/photos/schools/stan/genrel/auto_pdf/BCC-Benefits-chart.pdf>, (3/8/12).

Beyond these advantages, the affluent and their tax advisors over the years have shown remarkable ingenuity in devising ways of reducing their tax burdens while making contributions. For its part, Congress has responded by erecting restrictions on giving, whose primary effect is on high-income taxpayers, but these limits do not negate those three features of the law.

By virtue of their high incomes and these favorable tax features, the wealthy not only account for a vastly disproportionate share of the country's total charitable donations, but they also account for an even bigger share of tax subsidies for donations. As shown in table 3.4, individuals with incomes over $500,000, representing just 1% of all taxpayers and earning 18% of all income, accounted for almost a quarter of all contributions in 2008 (including those made by non-itemizers). By contrast, taxpayers with incomes under $50,000, who were almost two-thirds of all taxpayers, had about a fifth of the income and made about a fifth of all donations. To see that the distribution of tax subsidies was even more lopsided than the distribution of donations, consider the table's last column, showing the percentage of taxpayers in each income category who itemized their deductions. The table shows that only 15% of these under-$50,000 taxpayers were itemizers, implying that 85% of the taxpayers in that category received no subsidy at all. In contrast, virtually all those in the top categories itemized their deductions. Further differentiating the subsidies received at the top and bottom of the income scale is the fact that those at the top also faced higher marginal rates on average, making the subsidy per dollar given greater than for those who itemized in the bottom income category. In

Table 3.4 Share of Tax Returns, Income, and Contributions and Percent Itemizers, by Income, 2008

Adjusted gross income ($ thousands)	Income			Itemizers (%)
	Tax returns	Income	Contributions	
Under 50	65	21	19	15
50 to 100	22	27	24	58
100 to 200	10	22	21	86
200 to 500	2	12	12	96
Over 500	1	18	24	96
Total	100	100	100	34

Note: Percentage based on all taxpayers, except for percentages itemizing in two highest income groups, which are based on taxable returns only. Contributions include estimates of those by non-itemizers.

Source: Columns 1–3, US Congressional Budget Office, *Options for Changing the Tax Treatment of Charitable Giving* (May 2011, Table 1, p. 5); Column 4, *Statistics of Income, 2008*, Table 1.2.

2006 taxpayers with incomes over $100,000 received 76% of the total $40.9 billion tax subsidy due to the charitable deduction, although they made just 57% of all donations. In contrast, those with incomes less than $50,000 received just 5% of the subsidy, despite making 19% of all contributions (CBO 2011a, p. 4).[32]

These differences in the rate of tax subsidy across the income scale take on added significance when one considers the particular charitable tastes of the wealthy. As noted above, taxpayers with incomes over $1 million tend to favor higher education, health, and the arts. For the super-wealthy, these preferences are even more pronounced. An analysis of the 90 largest gifts in 1996, for example, showed a stunning 56% of the total going to higher education. In addition, 17% went to health organizations, 14% to arts and culture, and 8% to private foundations.[33] Patterns of charitable bequests by the wealthy lean heavily toward private foundations.[34] A tabulation for estates in 1995 showed that nearly three-quarters of bequests from estates over $20 million went to foundations. The wealthy have long occupied a prominent position in American philanthropy, of course, as seen in the foundations established by captains of industry such as Carnegie, Duke, and Rockefeller. Today's stars of industry and finance are no less prominent, and, indeed, discussion of "the 1%" is very prominent these days. One development of note, though, is a movement among some of America's wealthiest individuals to emulate those nineteenth century philanthropists by giving away most of their money. This movement has been formalized in the form of a public pledge to give a majority of their wealth to philanthropy in their lifetimes or after their death.[35] The very biggest donors, indeed, are in a class by themselves. Not surprisingly, they enjoy a disproportionate amount of influence in the governance of the nonprofit organizations receiving their donations. A glance at the board of directors of any large museum or private university, even the guest list in the president's box at a university's football stadium, will attest to this disproportionate influence. Arguably, their influence would be

[32] These figures, like those in table 3.4, are based on all taxpayers, not just those who itemized.

[33] See Clotfelter et al. (1997, Table 12.2, p. 406). For the most recent data on large gifts, see the Slate 60, <http://www.slate.com/articles/life/the_slate60/2011/02/the_2010_slate_60.html> (3/29/12). By comparison, charitable bequests reveal similar patterns, with private foundations accounting for the largest share for the very biggest estates. The shares of bequests in 2007 for estates of $3.5 million or more were: philanthropy, 56.5%; education, 12.3%; arts, 6.7%; human services, 4.9%; health and medical, 4.3%; religion, 4.2%; environment, 2.3%; and other, unknown, 8.8% (Raub, 2009).

[34] Auten, Clotfelter, and Schmalbeck (2000, p. 415).

[35] The Giving Pledge, <http://givingpledge.org/> (3/29/12). Michael Bloomberg, Warren Buffett, Paul Allen, Charles Feeney, Bill and Melinda Gates. T. Boone Pickens, Ted Turner.

large even if there were no charitable deduction, but US tax policy enhances that influence. What else do these big donors get in return for their big gifts? According to Ostrower (1995), philanthropy for the wealthy takes on considerable social significance, acting as a marker of elite status. Being identified as a member of this exclusive circle is strengthened by membership on boards and recognition at dinners, receptions, and other public events. Not only do they sit on governing boards and boards of visitors, but they are also invited to receptions, and singled out for recognition at public events. There are also naming opportunities, ranging from the scholarship or alcove worth a million dollars to having a building, or even a school, named after you. At one extreme, Odendahl (1989, p. 243) has argued that the wealthiest donors fund institutions from which they benefit and over which they exert great control: "Whether it be high culture, high education, or the high medicine of private nonprofit hospitals, the rich fund and make policy for these institutions, while, on the whole, the middle class produces the cultural and intellectual products and services."[36]

Although the charitable deduction has been justified on the basis that money given away is no longer available to the donor, and therefore should not be taxed as income, there are ways for donors, particularly wealthy ones, to retain considerable control even after the donation has been made. The most effective means of doing so is the private foundation. Subject to several limitations, most of which were imposed by the Congress in 1969, wealthy individuals can retain control over how their charitable funds are distributed to the ultimate charitable recipients simply by remaining in control of their own private foundation.[37] For less expense and trouble, donors with more modest means can likewise receive an immediate tax deduction while retaining some control over the disposition of funds by utilizing donor-advised funds, commonly overseen by community foundations and investment companies, or a so-called supporting organization, often established by large nonprofits like universities.[38] These latter two mechanisms also offer the taxpayer a

[36] Community leaders from the middle class may play similar leadership roles in local fundraising efforts. In their classic sociological study of American urban life in the 1920s, Lynd and Lynd (1929, p. 464) describe the launching of the community chest drive in Muncie, Indiana: "The first step was to enlist the big men in town, the Rotary crowd, as the responsible heads upon whom success or failure depended. There was the minimum of Christian *caritas* about it, no zeal for a particular emergency or needy family..."

[37] Among the limitations imposed on foundations are: a lower portion of income may be deducted for gifts to them; deductions of gifts of appreciated property to them are limited to the tax basis rather than their market value; a minimum of 5% of assets must be distributed each year; there are limitations on self-dealing; and there is an excise tax on investment income (Auten, Clotfelter, and Schmalbeck 2000, p. 397).

[38] See Auten, Clotfelter, and Schmalbeck (2000, p. 398). In recent years, Fidelity and other investment companies have made it easy for investors to set up donor-advised funds.

chance to smooth their giving over time when their income fluctuates from year to year. More commonly, large gifts often confer influence of an informal nature. Big donors may be rewarded, for example, with a seat on the museum's board of directors or the university's board of visitors.[39]

Americans often write in celebratory terms about the country's generosity and voluntary spirit, and indeed there is much that is admirable in the US system. But, as John Shoven (2000, pp. 425–6) has noted, one can question just how public-spirited some of this giving really is. Since donations are often used for things the government would not have purchased, it is natural to compare the public benefit of tax expenditures for donations with what those dollars would have paid for in the absence of the donation. Shoven's example is a $3 million bequest to pay for a fountain on a university campus. Shoven asks the question: Which taxpayer is more charitable, the one who makes the donation, thereby imposing all taxpayers to subsidize it, or the one who makes no donation, thus increasing total tax receipts by the amount that would otherwise have been forgone tax revenue? The answer will inevitably depend in part on one's comparison of the social value of the donation and that of the government's counterfactual expenditure. But suppose gridlock on Capitol Hill means that the kinds of international programs undertaken by the Gates Foundation can only be done through charitable contributions. Then Shoven's speculation could well be turned on its head, leading back to what has become one of the principal justifications for nonprofit organizations—that they plug holes in the provision of public goods left when both the market and government fail to supply them.[40] This example suggests the possibility of applying different rates of subsidy to different types of donations depending on the public benefit generated, an approach implied by some theoretical models (e.g., Saez 2004). The US tax law has largely sidestepped this issue, choosing instead to differentiate simply by allowing or disallowing gifts by type of organization. The result is that the tax system can end up subsidizing donations that yield little apparent public benefit.[41]

See Fidelity Charitable, <http://www.fidelitycharitable.org/giving-strategies/give/donor-advised.shtml> (5/2/12).

[39] See, for example, Meer and Rosen (2009), for an analysis of the behavior of alumni donors to a private university.

[40] For a cogent statement of this thesis, see Weisbrod (1988).

[41] One such category is donations to aid commercial college sports enterprises. See Charles Clotfelter, "Uncle Sam Takes one for the Team," *Washington Post*, December 31, 2010.

3.4 Ongoing Issues in US Tax Policy and Charitable Giving

Change could come about in US tax policy toward charitable giving, inadvertently or deliberately. As to the first, the treatment of contributions could find itself an innocent bystander affected by wider tax reform. Judging from the policy debates in Washington, the individual income tax, that reliable source of more federal revenue than any other source, has many critics but precious few admirers. Among the most frequent charges against it are that it is unnecessarily complex, that it taxes the rich too lightly, and that its many loopholes make it unfair and inefficient. At the same time, among the existing tax's many provisions, the deduction for charitable contributions does enjoy wide support, a fact that becomes evident as soon as someone proposes to simplify the income tax by getting rid of base-eroding loopholes, usually for the purpose of lowering tax rates. "Flat rate tax" schemes, a tax reform cottage industry in the 1980s, enjoyed a resurgence in 2012 with one presidential candidate's advocacy of a plan to tax income at a flat 9% rate.[42] The argument that the rich are taxed lightly, central to the opposition to extending the George W. Bush tax cuts for the high-income taxpayers, got a second wind thanks to billionaire Warren Buffett's complaint that he paid a lower income tax rate than his secretary.[43] The debate about fairness was also fueled by evidence showing that households at the very top of the income distribution were enjoying a growing share of the economic pie.[44] Whether any of these complaints would ultimately lead to tax reform was unclear, they bring to mind the quip that "skeptical politicians rank serious tax reform with gun control and free world trade—as worthy causes unworthy of the time of realists."[45] Yet major tax reform—incorporating changes in marginal tax rates or the charitable deduction itself—does occasionally happen, and when it does, it will inevitably affect donors' incentives to give.

Beyond the slim but ever-present possibility of fundamental reform, a second way tax treatment of charitable giving could change is by way of deliberate modification of the current deduction. One motivation for change is unhappiness with the whole upside-down nature of the existing subsidy. A straightforward remedy would be to replace the deduction with a credit that applies to all taxpayers. A less radical

[42] Herman Cains "999" plan was not a fully fleshed out proposal, however, as were some of the proposals of the 1980s, like the Hall-Rabuska Flat Tax; <http://www.hoover.org/publications/books/8329> (4/1/12).

[43] Warren E. Buffett, "Stop Coddling the Super-Rich," *New York Times*, August 14, 2011.

[44] Between 1977 and 2007, the share of total income going to households in the top 1% doubled, from 10% to 20% (CBO 2011b, p. xi).

[45] Editorial, "Yes, There Is a Better Income Tax," *New York Times*, June 6, 1982.

approach would be to cap the tax rate applied to the deduction, exemplified by the Obama Administration's proposal to limit itemized deductions to 28%, or to allow nonitemizers to deduct donations, as they could briefly, in 1986.[46] But in opposition to any expansion of the deduction are those who want to see the tax base expanded rather than narrowed. Thus one perennial idea is to permit a deduction, but only for donations that exceed a certain floor. Not only would a floor reduce the amount of revenue lost, it would also simplify tax compliance, since taxpayers giving less than the floor would not need to keep records. It would also eliminate at least one source of potentially questionable deductions, since the tax authorities currently have no way to verify small charitable contributions. A drawback to a floor is that some taxpayers would lose the tax incentive, at the margin, to donate, or might seek to bunch their gifts, for example, by donating every other year, so that they could deduct more of their giving, thus negating some of a floor's potential revenue savings. Such a floor (at 1% of income) was one of the reforms proposed by a prominent panel in 2005. The panel's other ideas for reforming the treatment of charitable contributions included mandating that charities report to the IRS all gifts over a certain size, reconsidering the kinds of organizations eligible to receive deductible gifts, and requiring the gains on gifts of appreciated property to be realized, while retaining the non-taxation of gains.[47]

To assess the likely effects of some of these reforms, the CBO recently produced projections based on simulated effects for individual taxpayers, using data for 2006. Presented in table 3.5, the first two show the projected effects of placing a floor beneath the current deduction. Imposing a $1,000 floor for joint returns ($500 for individuals) would, as expected, save revenue and discourage contributions, but imposing a much more stringent 2% of AGI floor would have much bigger effects, of both kinds.[48] Extending the deduction to nonitemizers would increase the tax subsidy by more than 10% but increase total giving by only 1%. The last four options included in the table show the effects of replacing the current deduction with a nonrefundable credit applied to all taxpayers. Contributions and total subsidy are predicted to rise in the case of a credit of 25% with no floor. The other three credit options show declines in both.

[46] Robert Frank, "Why Obamas Jobs Bill Could be Bad for Charity," *Wall Street Journal*, September 13, 2011.

[47] President's Advisory Panel on Federal Tax Reform (2005, pp. 75–8).

[48] Ackerman and Auten (2006) provide simulations for a 1% floor, which are similar to those produced by the CBO for a 2% floor.

Table 3.5 CBOs Predicted Effects for Eight Illustrative Tax Reforms, 2006 Levels

	Floor for donations?	Total contributions ($ billion)	Tax subsidy ($ billion)
		Current Law	
Deduction for itemizers only	No	203.0	40.9
		Changes from current Law	
Deduction for itemizers only	$500 / $1,000	−0.5	−5.6
Deduction for itemizers only	2% of AGI	−3.0	−15.7
Extend deduction to nonitemizers	No	2.0	5.2
Extend deduction to nonitemizers	2% of AGI	1.9	−13.1
Replace deduction with 25% credit	No	2.7	7.1
Replace deduction with 25% credit	2% of AGI	−1.0	−11.9
Replace deduction with 25% credit	No	−7.8	−13.3
Replace deduction with 25% credit	2% of AGI	−10.0	−24.6

Note: $500/$1,000 would be $500 for individual filers and $1,000 for joint filers. Credits would be non-refundable. Changes in contributions assume a price elasticity of –0.5.

Source: Congressional Budget Office (2011, Summary Table 1, p. ix).

Most of the tax policy issues applying to donations during life have a counterpart in the estate and gift tax with respect to charitable bequests. Only the aggregate dollar amounts of charitable bequests are much smaller. Whereas deductible contributions in the income tax were $158 billion in 2009, deductions for charitable bequests in estates were only about $20 billion.[49] To be sure, as noted above, the great bulk of charitable bequests are made by a tiny minority of decedents, and they are much more likely to go to private foundations or higher education than are contributions from the living. In 2012 the tax applied to estates of $5.12 million or more, with a rate of 35%. As with giving in life, bequest giving is thought to have a tax price effect.[50] So the vitriolic debate over the "death tax"—which could lead to an increased exemption, a lower rate of tax, or outright elimination—has the potential to leave a mark on charitable bequests. Econometric studies imply that eliminating the tax would result in declines in charitable bequests ranging from 20 to 37% (Joulfaian, 2009, p. 1227).[51]

[49] Deductions in individual income tax: US Internal Revenue Service, *Statistics of Income 2009*, Table 2.1; charitable bequests: $19.7 billion in 2007, <http://www.irs.gov/pub/irs-soi/07es01fy.xls> (4/8/12).

[50] I.R.S., Publication 950, *Introduction to Estate and Gift Taxes*, p. 4.

[51] For taxpayers with enough wealth to be subject to the estate tax, making donations in life has the extra tax benefit of reducing the taxable estate. Thus part of the observed tax effect on lifetime giving could be masking an estate tax effect as well.

3.5 Conclusion

Charitable contributions play a bigger role in the provision of public goods in the United States than in other developed countries. By allowing taxpayers to have a large role in allocating public subsidies, American tax law reflects a tradition of reliance on nonprofit organizations and individual choice, as opposed to tax-financed government provision. The centerpiece of US tax policy is a deduction for contributions to charitable, educational, and scientific nonprofit organizations, a feature that ends up subsidizing the gifts of high-income taxpayers the most, lower-income renters the least, and middle-class homeowners in the middle. One of the most significant consequences of this tax treatment of charitable giving is to give to the wealthiest taxpayers a disproportionate role in allocating public resources and influencing the direction that institutions will take. Within American policy, therefore, there exists an inherent conflict between participatory citizenship and elitism.

This tax treatment could change, for either of two reasons. First, tax reforms that modify the tax rate structure or the portion of taxpayers who itemize their deductions will necessarily affect the tax price of giving for some or many taxpayers. Second, any one of a number of reforms specifically related to charitable giving, such as applying a floor, could also affect the tax price of giving. These changes would affect not only the amount of revenue lost, but also, depending on the assumed behavioral parameters, the amount of donations made. In light of the budget pressure to raise revenues, it would not be surprising if one of these changes had been adopted by the time this volume goes to press. A floor on the charitable deduction is attractive because it will save time and revenue, depending on the amount of the floor, could have a minimal effect on charitable giving, since it would not affect the subsidy applied to the last dollar of giving. A limit on deductions, however, will have such an effect for taxpayers who are at the limit, thus removing the subsidy on donations at the margin. From the standpoint of economic efficiency, reforms that equalize subsidy rates across taxpayers, including a deduction for non-itemizers or a tax credit, would be attractive. Politically, the latter reform seems most unlikely.

Acknowledgments

I am grateful to Gerald Auten, Joel Fleishman, Kristin Goss, Ralph McCaughan, Edward Skloot, Larry Zelenak, and the editors for helpful comments and suggestions and to John Mcginty for research assistance. The views expressed are those of the author and do not necessarily represent those of any organization.

References

Ackerman, Deena and Gerald E. Auten (2006). "Floors, Ceilings, and Opening the Door for a Non-Itemizer Deduction," *National Tax Journal* 59, 509–30.

Ackerman, Deena and Gerald Auten (2008). "Tax Expenditures for Noncash Charitable Contributions," draft chapter presented at the NBER conference, "Incentive and Distributional Consequences of Tax Expenditures," March 27–9.

Alesina, Alberto, Edward Glaeser, and Bruce Sacerdote (2001). "Why Doesn't the United States Have a European-Style Welfare State?" *Brookings Papers on Economic Activity* 2, 1–69.

Andrews, William D. (1972). "Personal Deductions in an Ideal Income Tax," *Harvard Law Review* 86, 309–85.

Auten, Gerald E., Charles T. Clotfelter, and Richard L. Schmalbeck (2000). "Taxes and Philanthropy among the Wealthy," in Joel Slemrod (ed.), *Does Atlanta Shrug? The Economics Consequences of Taxing the Rich* (New York and Cambridge, MA: Russell Sage Foundation and Harvard University Press), pp. 392–424.

Auten, Gerald E., Holger Sieg, and Charles T. Clotfelter (2002). "Charitable Giving, Income and Taxes: An Analysis of Panel Data," *American Economics Review* 92, 371–82.

Auten, Gerald, James Cilke, and William Randolph (1992). "The Effects of Tax Reform on Charitable Contributions," *National Tax Journal* 45, 267–90.

Bakija, Jon and Bradley Heim (2011). "How Does Charitable Giving Respond to Incentives and Income? New Estimates for Panel Data," *National Tax Journal* 64, 615–50.

Bremner, Robert H. (1977). "Private Philanthropy and Public Needs: Historical Perspective," in Commission on Private Philanthropy and Public Needs, Research Papers, Vol. I (Washington: US Treasury Department).

Cabot, Tyler (2002). "The Tow-Away Tax Break: Why Car Donation Programs Benefit Everyone but the Charities They're Intended to Help," Washington Monthly, pp. 39–42.

CBD (US Congressional Budget Office) (2004). *The Estate Tax and Charitable Giving* (Washington: CBO).

CBD (US Congressional Budget Office) (2011a). *Options for Changing the Tax Treatment of Charitable Giving* (Washington: CBO).

CBD (US Congressional Budget Office) (2011b). *Trends in the Distribution of Household Income Between 1979 and 2007* (Washington: CBO).

Center on Philanthropy (2007). Indiana University, Patterns of Household Charitable Giving by Income Group 2005.

Clotfelter, Charles T. (1985). Federal Tax Policy and Charitable Giving (Chicago: University of Chicago Press).

Clotfelter, Charles T. (ed.) (1992). *Who Benefits from the Nonprofit Sector?* (Chicago: University of Chicago Press).

Clotfelter, Charles T. (1997). "The Economics of Giving," in John W. Barry and Bruno V. Manno (eds), *Giving Better, Giving Smarter:* Working Papers of the National Commission on Philanthropy and Civic Renewal (Washington, DC: National Commission on Philanthropy and Civic Renewal, 1997), pp. 31–55.

Clotfelter, Charles T. (2010). *American Universities in a Global Market* (Chicago: University of Chicago Press).

De Neubourg, Chris, Julie Castonguay and Keetie Roelen, (2007). "Social Safety Nets and Targeted Social Assistance: Lessons from the European Experience," Social Protection Discussion Paper 0718, World Bank.

Fack, Gabrielle and Camille Landais (2010). "Are Tax Incentives for Charitable Giving Efficient? Evidence from France," *American Economic Journal: Economic Policy*, 2(2): 117–141.

Giving USA, (2011). (Indianapolis: Center on Philanthropy, Indiana University, 2011).

Hammack, David C. (ed.) (1998). *Making the Nonprofit Sector in the United States* (Bloomington: Indiana University Press).

Howard, Christopher (1997). *The Hidden Welfare State: Tax Expenditures and Social Policy in the United States* (Princeton: Princeton University Press).

Joulfaian, David (2009). "On Estate Tax Repeal and Charitable Bequests," *Tax Notes*.

Lynd, Robert S. and Helen Merrell Lynd (1929). *Middletown: A Study in Contemporary American Culture* (New York: Harcourt, Brace and Company).

Marron, Donald (2011). "Spending in Disguise," *National Affairs*.

Meer, Jonathan and Harvey S. Rosen (2009). "Family Bonding with Universities," *NBER Working Paper* 15493. Cambridge, MA: NBER.

Odendahl, Teresa (1989). "The Culture of Elite Philanthropy in the Reagan Years," *Nonprofit and Voluntary Sector Quarterly* 18, 237–48.

OECD, OECD Factbook (2001). "Economic, Environmental and Social Statistics, Public and Private Social Expenditures," <http://dx.doi.org/10.1787/888932507103>.

Ostrower, Francie (1995). *Why the Wealthy Give: The Culture of Elite Philanthropy* (Princeton: Princeton University Press).

President's Advisory Panel on Federal Tax Reform (2005). Simple, Fair, and Pro-Growth: Proposal to Fix America's Tax System.

Prewitt, Kenneth (2006). "American Foundations: What Justifies Their unique Privileges and Powers," in Kenneth Prewitt et al. (eds), *The Legitimacy of Foundations: United States and European Perspectives* (New York: Russell Sage Foundation).

Raub, Brian (2009). "A Look at Estate Tax Returns Filed for Wealthy Decedents Since 2001," *Statistics of Income Bulletin*.

Saez, Emmanuel (2004). "The Optimal Treatment of Tax Expenditures," *Journal of Public Economics* 88, 2657–84.

Salamon, Lester M. (2003). *The Resilient Sector: The State of Nonprofit America* (Washington: Brookings Institution Press), pp. 27–46.

Shoven, John (2000). "Commentary on Chapter 12," in Joel Slemrod (ed.), *Does Atlanta Shrug? The Economics Consequences of Taxing the Rich* (New York and Cambridge MA: Russell Sage Foundation and Harvard University Press), pp. 425–6.

Smeeding, Timothy (2006). "Poor People in Rich Nations: The United States in Comparative Perspective," *Journal of Economic Perspectives* 20, 69–90.

US Office of Management and Budget (2010). *Fiscal Year 2012 Budget of the US Government* (Washington: Government Printing Office).

Weisbrod, Burton (1988). *The Nonprofit Economy* (Cambridge, MA: Harvard University Press).

Wing, Kennard T., Thomas H. Pollak, and Amy Blackwood (2008). *The Nonprofit Almanac* (Washington: Urban Institute Press).

Yermack, David (2009). "Deductio ad absurdum: CEOs Donating their Own Stock to their Own Family Foundations," *Journal of Financial Economics* 94, 107–23.

4

Philanthropy, Tax Policy, and Tax Cheating: A Long-Run Perspective on US data

Gabrielle Fack & Camille Landais

4.1 Introduction

Tax incentives for charitable giving have existed in the US federal income tax system since 1917. In 2007, US taxpayers reported in their income tax returns a total of \$193.6 Bn in charitable contributions. This figure represents 2.2% of total adjusted gross income (AGI). The basis for subsidizing private charitable contributions is indeed well established: Private charitable contributions finance many socially valuable activities (education, the arts, nonprofits, religious organizations, and so forth) and therefore have a positive external effect that can be encouraged with Pigouvian subsidization. Nevertheless, there still exists a substantial debate over the optimal level of the subsidy rate. The presidential administration of Barack Obama introduced a proposal that capped the subsidy rate for the top income-earning households. Other countries, such as France, have recently considerably increased the level of the tax subsidy for contributions in order to boost private provision of public goods (Fack and Landais, 2010). Policy recommendations in the debate over the optimal level of the subsidy rely on a large body of theoretical and empirical work (see Andreoni, 2006 for a complete survey). Yet this literature focuses almost exclusively on a single parameter, the price elasticity of contributions, which is implicitly assumed to be a sufficient statistic to infer tax policy.[1]

Surprisingly, there is very little discussion in the literature that the federal income tax deduction for charitable contributions is also an easy channel for tax evasion because of the permissive tax enforcement regime applicable to charitable gifts. Some studies have nevertheless shown that tax cheating may be a concern. Ackerman and Auten (2008) investigate contributions of used cars and find evidence of significant overvaluation of used cars by donors on their tax forms. Yermack (2008) analyzes contributions of stocks by CEOs to their own private foundations and finds that these gifts, which are not subject to insider trading laws, often occur just before sharp declines in their companies' share prices, suggesting that some CEOs backdate stock gifts to increase personal income tax benefits. Slemrod (2006) and Feldman and Slemrod (2007) also try to measure tax evasion occurring through charitable deductions with audited and unaudited tax returns, respectively. But overall, there has been no general investigation into the extent of tax cheating through private charitable contributions, nor has there been any attempt to understand to what extent tax cheating may modify our normative approach to subsidizing private philanthropy.

The aim of this chapter is to twofold. First we show for the first time evidence of substantial behavioral responses of wealthy taxpayers to charitable giving deductions in a very long time perspective. Second, we show that part of this response may be due to tax cheating. We develop a model of tax cheating and show that tax cheating is a first-order phenomenon to assess optimal tax policies for charitable contributions. Then, we unveil the existence of substantial tax evasion carried out through charitable deductions using a natural experiment on tax enforcement in the US.

We begin our chapter with the estimation of the price elasticity of reported contributions. We improve on previous research by building a long-term dataset of contributions and marginal tax rates for top incomes in the United States since 1917. The creation of this long-term dataset offers several advantages for our purposes. First, it gives us the opportunity to address the simultaneity issue of variations in price and income. By using many more legislative changes of the income tax schedule than did previous tax studies, we obtain substantial price variations over time affecting differently different income groups. This enables us to create several instruments for price and income variations.

[1] Crowding-out parameters (the extent to which public provision of a public good crowds-out private contributions to the public good) have also received some attention (see Warr (1982), Kingma (1989), or Gruber and Hungerman (2007) for instance).

In addition, we can control for differential trends in giving across groups and investigate dynamic issues, such as state dependence or time shifting of contributions. Our results demonstrate that the long-term price elasticity of contributions in the United States is inferior to one in absolute value but not significantly different from one for the top 0.1% of taxpayers. However, these policy recommendations become very misleading in the presence of tax cheating.

In order to derive policy recommendation in the presence of tax cheating, we develop a general framework to define the sufficient statistics to be estimated to assess the optimality of tax subsidies for contributions in the presence of tax cheating. Our optimal tax formula generalizes to the case of tax cheating the unit elasticity rule, which assumes that the price elasticity of reported contributions is a sufficient statistic to infer tax policy. Our results show that, in the presence of tax cheating, three welfare-sufficient statistics must be estimated to assess tax subsidy optimality for charitable contributions. These statistics are the price elasticity of reported contributions, the share of contributions that is cheated, and the price elasticity of cheating contributions. These results can be compared with those of Chetty (2009a) which demonstrates that, in the presence of tax sheltering, the taxable income elasticity is no longer a welfare-sufficient statistic to calculate deadweight loss, which becomes a weighted average of taxable income and full income elasticities.

We then show evidence of cheating behaviors in the United States. We focus on a natural experiment that significantly modified tax enforcement of contributions to private foundations. In 1969, Congress passed a law preventing "self-dealing" and other possibilities for abuses through contributions to private foundations. Annual creation of private foundations dropped by more than 80% between 1968 and 1970 suggesting that private foundations were largely used as tax sheltering vehicles. Moreover, the reform lowered incentives to cheat as it pertained to rich taxpayers who had private foundations, but did not affect taxpayers at lower levels of income. We therefore use a standard difference-in-difference strategy, and look at the effect of the reform on contributions reported by the top 0.01% of taxpayers relative to contributions of other top income groups not rich enough to set up their own private foundations. The results suggest that a very significant fraction (around 30%) of contributions reported by the very wealthy before 1969 were driven by tax avoidance or tax cheating purposes. We then use these estimates to calibrate our model.

The chapter is organized as follows. Section 4.2 presents long-run data on philanthropy in the US, and corresponding estimates of elasticity of charitable giving. Next, we show how these statistics can be misleading in the presence of tax cheating and develop a general model of optimal subsidy in the presence of tax cheating. We then present our natural experiment of tax enforcement and use it to calibrate our model and discuss optimal tax policy in the presence of tax cheating.

4.2 The Long-run of Charitable Contributions by the Very Wealthy

4.2.1 *Elasticity of Reported Contributions: Long-term Perspective*

Tax incentives for charitable giving have existed in the US federal income tax system since 1917. The system works as a deduction from taxable income of the amount of private contributions. The subsidy rate for a contribution is therefore equal to the marginal tax rate faced by a taxpayer, and we define the *price* of a contribution as $1 - \tau$, where τ is the marginal tax rate of the taxpayer. Since the seminal work of Feldstein and Taylor (1976), a wide range of empirical studies have focused on the estimation of price elasticity of charitable contributions. Nevertheless, there are sizeable differences in the estimates produced by these studies due to several empirical issues on US microdata.

The first issue to cope with is that of simultaneity of price and income variations. Early studies (such as Feldstein and Taylor, 1976), use cross-sectional data to estimate both price and income elasticities of charitable giving. They find that the elasticity of giving with respect to the tax-defined price is greater than one in absolute value, suggesting a high responsiveness to tax incentives. However, these early studies were plagued by identification problems caused by the simultaneous variations of income and price of giving. Since the deduction rate is equal to the marginal tax rate in the United States, and is therefore a function of income, it is difficult to disentangle the effect of a change in income from the effect of a change in price. Studies on panel data (including Randolph, 1995, Barett, McGuirk, and Steinberg 1997, and Bakija, 2000) have tried several methods to separately estimate the transitory changes in prices caused by fluctuations in income and the permanent changes in prices (for a review of studies that use US data, see Bakija and Heim, 2011). When breaking down income and prices in transitory and permanent components, Randolph finds estimates of the elasticity of giving with respect to the permanent price of giving ranging from −0.3 to −0.5, which is much lower than earlier findings. However, Auten, Sieg, and Clotfelter 2002, relying on a different method to identify transitory and permanent income shocks,[2] find higher permanent price elasticities, ranging from −0.79 to −1.26, and lower transitory elasticities than other studies. Fack and Landais (2010) overcome this problem of simultaneity in price and income variation by focusing on the French income tax credit for charitable contributions, whereby every taxpayer gets the same subsidy rate, and find much smaller price elasticity estimates than previous studies on US data. Second, identification in these studies is essentially brought by legislated tax changes that affect differently different income groups. Most studies focus on recent data with few tax changes. Therefore, one needs to assume that there are no differential trends in giving across groups. This is a standard identification problem in empirical tax studies, as shown by Saez, Slemrod, and Giertz (2009). In addition, studies such as Bakija and Heim (2011) have shown that sizeable short-term responses due to time shifting of reported contributions may occur, with the consequence of largely overstating the estimate of the long-term price elasticity of contributions. Finally, Bradley, Holden, and McLelland (2005) and Fack and Landais (2010) show that censoring/selection may severely affect the estimation of the elasticity of charitable giving in samples in which a significant portion of households do not contribute or do not itemize deductions.

Overall, empirical studies on the price elasticity of charitable giving have so far produced mixed results. If a consensus seems to have emerged that price elasticity is inferior to one in absolute value for the population of taxpayers as a whole, heterogeneity according to income appears to be large. In particular, it appears that the value of price elasticity rises with income, but little is known about the true value of the price elasticity among top-income households, because sources of identification at the very top of the income distribution have been scarce.[3] Here, we improve on previous literature by building a long-term dataset of contributions and marginal tax rates for top incomes in the US since 1917 that offers a large number of variations in marginal tax rates among taxpayers at the very top of the income distribution.

[2] They work directly on the variance-covariance matrix of income and prices and assume that these variables experience both random persistent shocks and transitory shocks that disappear after one year.

[3] Bakija and Heim (2011) use a panel of taxpayers spanning the years 1979 to 2005 that oversamples high income households. Our longer panel allows us to track changes in marginal tax rate of the top bracket over a century, including the high increase in the 1940s–1950s and the decrease in the 1970s–1980s.

DATA & STRATEGY

Data on contributions for 1917 to 1960 come from the published *Statistics of Income* (*SOI*) of the Internal Revenue Service (IRS). We interpolated charitable contributions from yearly tabulations of exhaustive reported contributions by income bracket to compute the evolution of total reported contributions of various stable income groups among top income households (the top decile of taxpayers since 1917).[4] For 1960 to 2005, we used yearly samples of microdata from the IRS with oversampling of high-income households. To compute long-term time series on effective marginal tax rates since 1917, we created a federal income tax simulator to compute effective marginal tax rates on earned income and on capital gains for top income groups, taking into account all reported income and deductions interpolated from yearly *SOI* tabulations. To the best of our knowledge, this is the first time such a simulator has been created, and it can now be used for several historical tax studies. For 1960 to 2005, we computed effective marginal tax rates from IRS microdata using the tax simulator of the National Bureau of

[4] Note that since 1944 the US offer to their taxpayers a choice between taking itemized deductions (including charity), or a standard deduction. As a result, tax return data in the US only provides information on the charitable donations of people who choose to itemize their deductions, which introduces a bias in the estimates of overall donations. The reason is that the decision to itemize is endogenously related to the size of one's charitable donation. People with unusually large charitable donations are more likely to itemize than people with similar characteristics but with smaller itemized deductions, because the former group is more likely to have itemized deductions that exceed the standard deduction. The extent to which this biases estimates of mean charitable donations by income class and year varies greatly by income class and by year. The bias is much more extreme at lower income levels, because people with lower incomes are far less likely than higher income people to have non-charitable itemized deductions large enough to exceed the standard deduction, and those that do not tend to have non-charitable itemized deductions tend to be further below the standard deduction threshold. Thus, for low- and middle-income people, data on charitable donations from US tax return data is really only representative of people who are at the extreme right-end tail of the generosity distribution. By contrast, higher income people are far more likely than lower- income people to have non-charitable itemized deductions that exceed the standard deduction, so that statistics on charitable donations by high-income itemizers will be representative of a much broader slice of the generosity distribution. To alleviate this issue, two solutions can be implemented. First, when microdata is available (for years 1960 and after in the United States for instance), one can compute contributions as a fraction of total income for exogenous itemizers in each income group, where exogenous itemizers are defined as individuals who have non-charitable itemized deductions that exceed the standard deduction. One can then use these observations to construct a correction factor to adjust the series when no microdata is available. The correction factor can be income-group specific (to take care of the fact that the itemization issue is likely to be a little more severe for individuals in the lower half of the top decile of richest taxpayers). The correction factor can also be made dependent on the ratio of the standard deduction to the average income in the income group, to take care of the fact that as the standard deduction increases (as a fraction of income), the probability to itemization will decrease for any level of contributions. A second, more straightforward way of alleviating the issue is to focus on top income groups, for which the fraction of itemizers is very large.

Economic Research (NBER), *Taxsim9*. Further details on the series can be found in Appendix 4.A.

The creation of this long-term dataset offers several advantages. First, it gives us the opportunity to address the simultaneity issue of variations in price and income. Using numerous legislated changes of the income tax schedule over time affecting differently different income groups, we create several instruments for price and income variations. Our first instrument for the price faced by a given income group at time t is the price for a synthetic level of income calculated as a times the average income, a being the long-term ratio (computed over the century) of the average income of the group divided by the average income in the population. We also use as an instrument the price of a contribution at the level of income of year n – 1 inflated by the *CPI* between year $n-1$ and year n. Focusing on data aggregated at the income group level is also useful, because we can assume that mean reversion effects are averaged out at the (aggregate) income group level, as opposed to panel data analysis in which sophisticated treatments of transitory price and income variations are needed. These mean reversion effects can be very important, like in the taxable income elasticity literature (Saez, Slemrod, and Giertz (2009)), and this is the reason why different ways to control for them in panel data analysis lead to substantial differences in the estimates of Auten et al. (2002) and Randolph (1995). Note that with data aggregated at the income group level, censoring issues are also alleviated, and the effect that we estimate is a mixture of responses at both the intensive and the extensive margins. In addition, our long-term dataset enables us to investigate dynamic issues. The numerous legislated tax changes spanned by our dataset allow us to include differential trends across income groups without destroying identification. We also look for time shifting behaviors by including the potential effects of lagged and forward variations in price due to anticipated changes in the legislation. Finally, we control for possible state dependence of contributions at the income group level with Blundell–Bond estimation models (Blundell and Bond (1998)) in which we allow contributions to follow an autoregressive process of order p.

Our baseline specification can be summarized as follows.

$$log(contribution)_{i,t} = \sum_i \alpha_i + \sum_t \theta_t + \epsilon log(price_{it}) + \beta log(income_{it}) + \varepsilon_{i,t} \tag{4.1}$$

where α_i are 6 income groups fixed effects and θ_t are year fixed effects. $income_{i,t}$ is the average gross income of the income group minus the average income tax computed without the benefit of the charitable deduction. Note that since 1917, taxpayers can deduct gifts of assets in the US federal tax system and that the implicit capital gain on the asset donated is not subject to tax. To control for this, we computed the price variables as follows:

$$price_{it} = 1 - mtr_{earned\ income} - \eta_{it} * s_{it} * mtr_{kgains}$$

η_{it} is the percentage appreciation of contributed asset relative to purchase price. Since we do not have information on η in our data, we rely on Bakija and Heim (2011) who estimated it to be 0.65, on average, based on Alternative Minimum Tax returns from 1989 to 1992. s_{it} is the share of asset contributions in total contributions. s_{it} may be endogenously correlated to the difference between the marginal tax rate on capital gain and the marginal tax rate on earned income. To avoid this issue, we use the long-term average of the share of asset contribution for each income group, $\overline{s_{it}}$. mtr_{kgains} is the marginal tax rate on capital gains, and $mtr_{earned\ income}$ is computed as the marginal tax rate on taxable earned income, not taking into account the deduction for charitable contributions.

RESULTS

Our long-term data bring some interesting new findings. Figures 4.1 to 4.4 display the main aspects of the long-term evolution of marginal tax rates and contributions. Figure 4.1 shows the long-term evolution of contributions as a percentage of total income in the United States for three income groups among the top decile of taxpayers since 1917. Two points are noteworthy. First, the variations in reported contributions for the top 10% to top 1% and for the top 1% to top 0.01% have been quite modest, compared with the variations experienced by the top 0.01% of taxpayers. Second, the top 0.01% of taxpayers have demonstrated very significant variations in reported contributions over the century, with a dramatic increase from the early 1930s to the late 1960s, and then a significant decrease. Figure 4.2 suggests that the surge in contributions by the top 0.01% of taxpayers from the early 1930s to the late 1960s is correlated with the dramatic increase in marginal tax rates for these top income taxpayers to levels as high as 90% in the mid-1940s. As can be seen in figures 4.3 and 4.4, it appears that the overall responsiveness of charitable contributions to marginal tax rates is less important when considering the entire top decile of taxpayers.

Table 4.1 displays estimation results for the top decile over the century. The main finding is that the overall price elasticity is inferior to one in absolute value in the very long term, and equal to about −0.6,

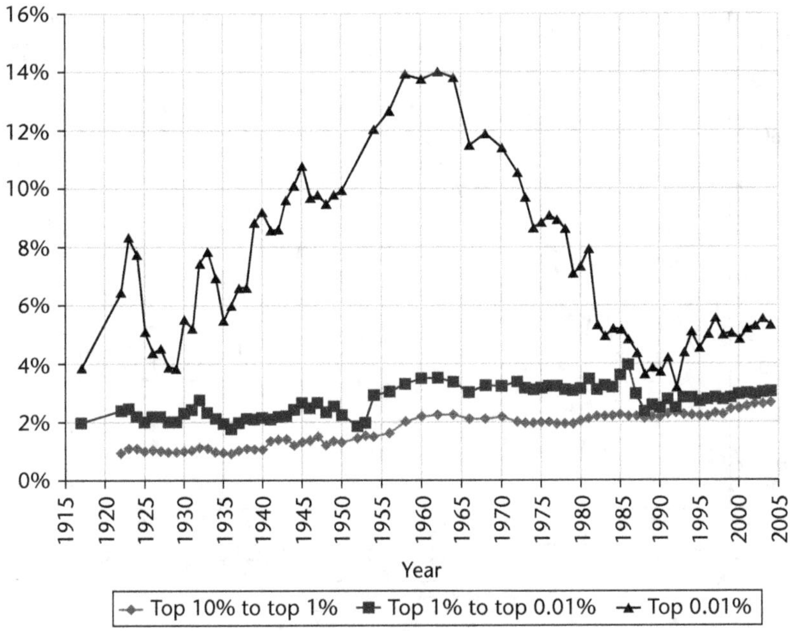

Figure 4.1 Charitable Contributions as a Percentage of Total Income for Top Income Groups. United States, 1917–2005

Notes: All series show reported donations for top income groups as a fraction of total income excluding capital gains.

Sources: Authors' computation from income tax statistics.

meaning that on average over the century, a 1% increase in the price of giving for top income groups has translated into a reduction in contributions of approximately 0.6%. This baseline estimate is very robust to the use of different instruments. Column (3) displays results of the specification in which *log(price)* is instrumented by the log of the price computed at *a* times the average income among all US taxpayers, *a* being the long-term ratio (averaged over the century) of the average income of the income group divided by the average income among all US taxpayers. Column (4) displays the results using as an instrument the log of the price computed at the average income level of the group in year $n-1$, inflated by the consumer price index variation between year $n-1$ and year n. To control for possible simultaneous variations of income and price in year n due to labor supply responses (or due to other types of income reporting responses to tax rate variations) we also instrument income in year n by the inflated income of year $n-1$. Results are displayed in column (5). In all cases, the value

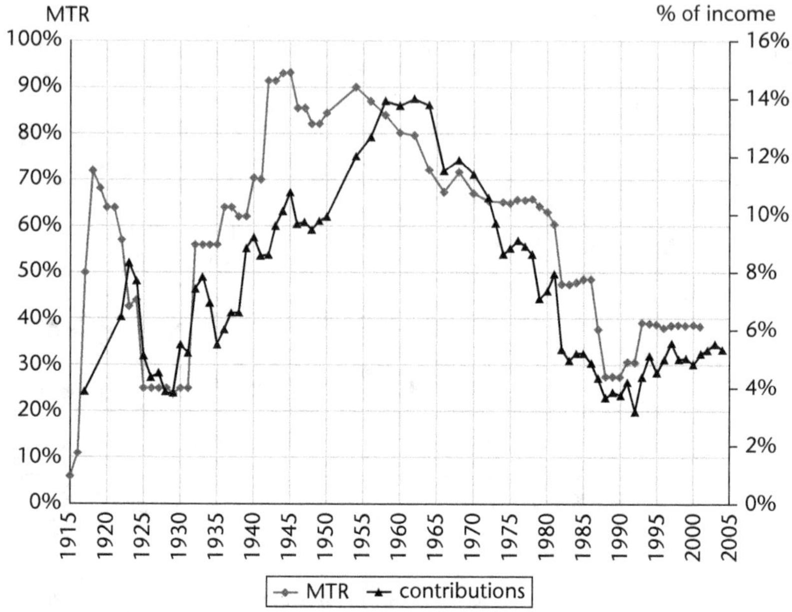

Figure 4.2 Effective Marginal Tax Rates and Reported Donations as a Fraction of Total Income for Top 0.01% of Richest Taxpayers in the US, 1917–2005

Notes: Contribution series show reported donations for top income groups as a fraction of total income excluding capital gains. Effective marginal tax rates series come from authors' historical tax simulator before 1960 and NBER TAXSIM after 1960 (see Appendix 4).

Sources: Authors' computation from income tax statistics.

of the elasticity is stable around –0.6. Note also that the income elasticity is very close to one, suggesting that private contributions can be considered as a normal good. This result is also robust across all specifications.

An important point to acknowledge is that since the 1970s, the large decline in marginal tax rates at the top of the distribution happened to coincide with a massive increase in the real disposable incomes of people at the top of the income distribution. This negative correlation between marginal tax rates and top income shares observed in the time series since the mid-1970s is a potentially confounding factor for our analysis. To alleviate this concern, table 4.1 does estimate the model for years 1917–2004. In the first half of the century, the correlation between top income shares and top marginal tax rates was much less strong, which should mitigate the problem. Note that alternative sensitivity analysis could also help address this concern. Bakija and

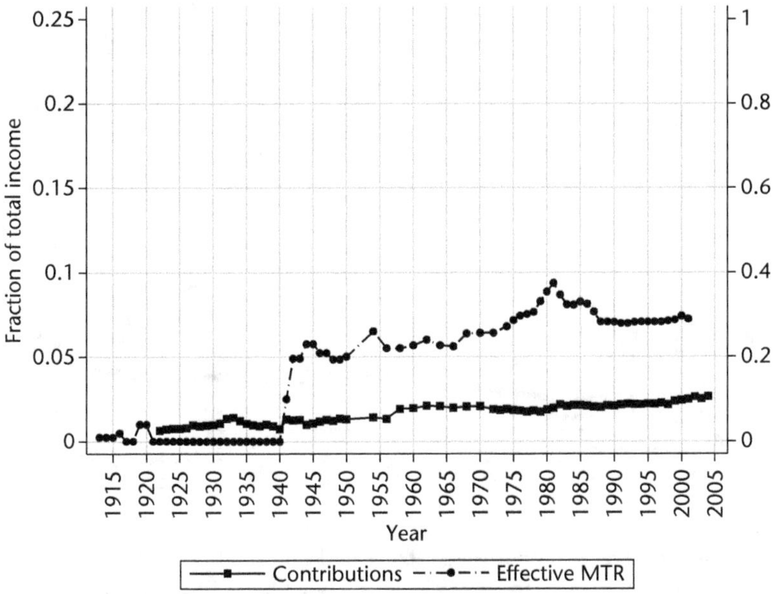

Figure 4.3 Effective MTR on Earned Income and Contributions as Percentage of Total Income. Top 10% to Top 5% (P90–95) Defined Excluding K Gains

Sources: Authors' computation from own tax simulator for years prior to 1962 and from the Taxsim9 simulator for years after 1960. MTR are federal marginal income tax rates on net earned income for the primary earner. For the years prior to 1960, MTR are computed for a couple filing jointly with two children and earning the average gross income in the income group, as interpolated from *SOI* tabulations. All adjustments and deductions are taken into account and are computed as average adjustments/deductions reported for the income group, as interpolated from *SOI* tabulations. Tax credits are not taken into account.

Heim (2011) for instance use data organized in narrow real disposable income ranges, rather than in income groups defined as fractiles of the income distribution.

As highlighted by our model, we have strong reasons to believe that the price elasticity of contributions is very sensitive to different tax enforcement regimes. Therefore, we concentrate in table 4.2 on the tax enforcement regime of years 1970 to 2004. The rules applicable for tax filing, for the ceiling of the deduction as a percentage of income, and for gifts of assets and to private foundations were stable over this period.[5] The results in table 4.2 demonstrate that the price elasticity of reported contributions has been around –0.6 for the top decile

[5] There is only one change: the brief inclusion as an Alternative Minimum Tax preference between 1986 and 1992 of unrealized capital gains on donations of some classes of appreciated assets.

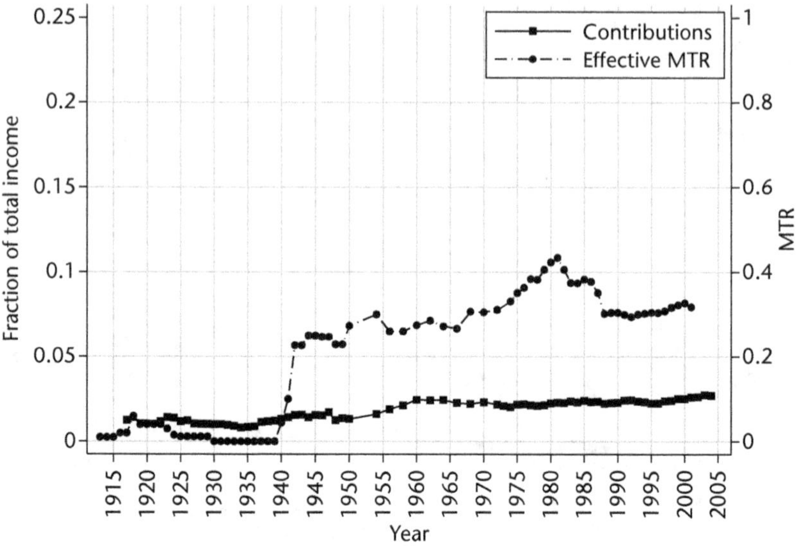

Figure 4.4 Effective MTR on Earned Income and Contributions as Percentage of Total Income. Top 5% to Top 1% (P95–P99) Defined Excluding K Gains

Sources: Authors' computation from own tax simulator for years prior to 1962 and from the Taxsim9 simulator for years after 1960. MTR are federal marginal income tax rates on net earned income for the primary earner. For the years prior to 1960, MTR are computed for a couple filing jointly with two children and earning the average gross income in the income group, as interpolated from *SOI* tabulations. All adjustments and deductions are taken into account and are computed as average adjustments/deductions reported for the income group, as interpolated from *SOI* tabulations. Tax credits are not taken into account.

Table 4.1 Price Elasticity Estimates, P90–100, 1917–2004

	(1) OLS fe	(2) OLS weighted	(3) IV fe	(4) IV fe	(5) IV fe
logprice	−0.649***	−0.683***	−0.595***	−0.620**	−0.658***
	(0.0941)	(0.0764)	(0.0975)	(0.219)	(0.0826)
logincome	0.965**	1.024**	0.914***	0.938***	1.032***
	(0.178)	(0.150)	(0.212)	(0.251)	(0.180)
Year fixed effects	YES	YES	YES	YES	YES
N	407	407	407	407	407

col. (2) OLS f.e. weighted by share of the group in total contrib.
col. (3) logprice instrumented by logprice at a * (average income). a = long-term ratio of mean income of the group divided by mean income of the pop.
col. (4) logprice instrumented by logprice at inflated income of year n − 1
col. (5) logincome instrumented by inflated reported income of year n − 1.

Clustered robust s.e. in parentheses. * $p < 0.05$, ** $p < 0.01$, *** $p < 0.001$
Income groups: P90–P95, P95–P99, P99–P99.95, P99.95–P99.99, P99.99–100.
P90: 90th percentile of the income distribution excluding K gains.

Table 4.2 Dynamic Panel Model Estimates P90–100, 1970–2004

	Top 10%			Top 10 to top 1%		Top 1%	
	IV fe (1)	IV fe (2)	IV Bl.-Bond (3)	IV fe (4)	IV fe (5)	IV fe (6)	IV fe (7)
logprice	−0.738***	−0.661***	−0.648***	−0.391	−0.159	−0.915***	−0.749***
	(0.153)	(0.0832)	(0.124)	(0.357)	(0.194)	(0.150)	(0.148)
Δ_t.logprice	0.322			0.856		0.447	
	(0.185)			(1.116)		(0.349)	
Δ_{t+1}.logprice	0.142			−0.620		−0.000123	
	(0.135)			(0.690)		(0.159)	
logincome	0.783***	0.531***	0.799***	0.542	0.610	0.859***	0.441**
	(0.0761)	(0.0870)	(0.0812)	(0.328)	(0.342)	(0.115)	(0.136)
logcontrib_{t-1}			0.342***				
			(0.0890)				
logcontrib_{t-2}			−0.0719**				
			(0.0241)				
logcontrib_{t-3}			−0.0548*				
			(0.0267)				
logcontrib_{t-4}			0.0789				
			(0.0793)				
logcontrib_{t-5}			0.0260				
			(0.0486)				
Year FE	YES	YES	YES	YES	YES	YES	YES
Trends interacted with group FE		YES			YES		YES
N	192	198	168	64	66	128	132

Cluster-robust standard errors in parentheses; * $p < 0.05$, ** $p < 0.01$, *** $p < 0.001$
Column (3): Blundell-Bond estimator. We allow contributions to follow an AR(5) process.

of US taxpayers for 1970 to 2004, which is very similar to the price elasticity computed for 1917 to 2004. This estimate is robust to the inclusion of controls for short-term shifting behaviors and of controls for differential trends in giving across income groups. In column (3), we control for state dependence by allowing contributions to follow an AR(5) process, and estimate the model with the Blundell and Bond estimator (Blundell and Bond (1998)). We also allow in this model errors to be serially correlated by assuming that errors follow a MA(1) process. The estimated price elasticity in this model is very similar to the previous estimates. Note that the coefficient on the first three lags of contributions are significant, implying that contributions are somehow state-dependent, but this does not affect our estimates of the price elasticity.

In columns (4) to (7) of table 4.2, we look at the heterogeneity of the price elasticity among income groups. First, we focus on the top 10% to top 1% income groups and find that the point estimates for the price elasticity are significantly lower than the average price elasticity for the entire top decile. Columns (6) and (7) confirm that the price elasticity is larger for the top 1% of taxpayers. Note that identification is still possible among the top 1% of taxpayers because this top percentile is broken down in four income groups in our data that experienced significantly different evolution of marginal tax rates over the period, as confirmed by data in table 4.7. The estimated elasticity for the top 1% of taxpayers is around −0.75 to −0.9 and not significantly different from one. Various reasons may explain why contributions of households at the very top of the income distribution are more responsive to taxation. Tax rates being higher in general for these taxpayers, tax rate variations may be more salient for these taxpayers than for taxpayers with lower income. Another reason is that taxpayers at the top of the income distribution have access to complicated tax cheating technologies. We argue in the following sections that "cheating" contributions may actually represent a significant fraction of contributions reported by the highest-income households.

4.3 Charitable Giving Policy in the Presence of Tax Cheating

4.3.1 *A Model of Optimal Subsidy in the Presence of Tax Cheating*

This section analyzes how tax cheating modifies the optimal treatment of tax expenditures. We focus on the case of the optimal level of a subsidy for charitable contributions. We begin by explaining the intuition behind our model in the simple case of a pure public finance objective in which the government seeks to maximize the amount of private contributions, given the public finance cost of the subsidy. Then we move to a more general model of optimal subsidy with warm-glow of giving (Andreoni, 2006) and crowding-out of private contributions through direct provision of the public good (Kingma, 1989). We derive a formula indicating the welfare-sufficient statistics to be estimated to assess the optimality of the subsidy rate in the presence of tax cheating.

The positive external effects of charitable contributions may justify tax incentives towards charitable giving, and numerous empirical studies have analyzed the effect of tax subsidies towards private philanthropy. However, the normative side of the analysis has been much less investigated,[6] and the issue of tax avoidance through charitable deduction has been even less investigated.[7]

Our model builds on the approach developped by Saez (2004) for the optimal treatment of tax expenditures in order to investigate the consequences of tax cheating on the optimal subsidy for charitable contributions. The distinction between illegal evasion and legal avoidance is not critical for our analysis: the term *cheating* is used as a general description of all evasion and avoidance behaviors that consist in using the charitable deduction for items that do not produce any positive externality.[8] Issues of tax evasion and tax avoidance have received growing attention in tax studies ever since the seminal work of Allingham and Sandmo (1972). Andreoni, Erard, and Feinstein

[6] Atkinson (1983) analyzes the optimal tax problem with a log functional form specification for the utility function in a model in which high-income households want to redistribute income to lower-income households. He then uses his optimal tax formula to study whether a deduction is more socially desirable than a flat-rate tax credit. Roberts (1987) investigates the issue of crowding-out of private contributions by direct public provision of a public good and derives a formula to determine whether direct funding of a public good via tax revenue is more desirable than subsidies to private contributions. Diamond (2006) analyzes the optimal subsidy for private donations in a nonlinear income tax schedule. His paper explores optimal policy, using first a model with standard preferences and then a model with warm-glow of giving. Diamond's paper emphasizes an important point for welfare analysis with the warm-glow model of giving, namely, that the optimal policy with warm-glow preferences is highly sensitive to the choice of preferences that are relevant for a social welfare evaluation. Indeed, one may consider that including warm-glow preferences in the social welfare function is somehow double-counting the utility gain of contributions for individuals. This is a standard problem encountered in welfare analysis with nonstandard preferences (such as hyperbolic discounting models, for instance) as underlined by Bernheim (2008). Here we abstract from these issues and consider the warm-glow motive as part of the preferences to be included in the social welfare function. Saez (2004) considers a very generalized model of optimal subsidy with a linear income tax and direct provision of public good by the government.

[7] Slemrod (2006) is the only paper, to our knowledge, that has analyzed the normative consequences of tax cheating, by stressing out that the traditional analysis of the efficiency of charitable deductions was not valid anymore in the presence of tax cheating.

[8] The fact that the distinction between avoidance and evasion is not necessarily relevant for deadweight loss analysis was already underlined by Chetty (2009a).

(1998) and Slemrod and Stephan (2007) survey this literature. But, apart from Slemrod (2006), who shows that in the presence of tax evasion, Feldstein's *unit elasticity rule* does not hold, the normative implications of avoidance have never been raised for the analysis of the optimal policy for charitable contributions. Here, however, for the sake of simplicity, we do not model the tax enforcement technology per se, contrary to most models of tax evasion in which the level of evasion chosen at the individual's optimum depends on the probability of being detected, which varies with the tax enforcement technology. We investigate the optimality of the subsidy rate *for a given level of tax enforcement*. Two important reasons explain why we abstract from modeling the tax enforcement technology. First, we are mainly interested in the level of the optimal subsidy rate.[9] Second, the choice of the tax enforcement regime is by itself not a critical question, because one tax enforcement regime strictly dominates all the others, namely, *third-party reporting* of charitable contributions by nonprofit organizations. The technology for third-party reporting is in fact already in place, making a switch to this regime virtually free of cost.[10] And as shown by Kleven et al. (2011) and Kleven, Kreiner, and Saez (2009), cheating behaviors are close to zero with third-party reporting. Of course, greater enforcement might also entail nonpecuniary social costs, such as invasion of privacy (Slemrod (2006)) that we do not take into account here, but that may partly explain why third-party reporting is not yet generalized.

A SIMPLE CASE: UNIT ELASTICITY RULE WITH AND WITHOUT TAX CHEATING

To explain how tax cheating affects the optimal tax policy for charitable contributions, we begin by focusing on a simple case of objective function in which the government only seeks to maximize the amount of private contributions, given the cost of the subsidy. This simple, objective function is actually not very far from what most governments have in mind when modifying the level of the subsidy rate, as shown

[9] Moreover, it is hard to consider tax enforcement technology as a well-behaved function of audit rates, as most models do. Tax enforcement is fundamentally discontinuous in the case of charitable giving and depends on different reporting regimes (whether households must keep receipts, can give away assets, can give to their private foundations, etc.).

[10] The UK system has indeed already a third-party reporting system for a large share of charitable contributions: through the gift aid scheme charities are entitled to reclaim a part of the tax paid by contributors, while taxpayers can reclaim the other part of the tax. This generates third-party reporting of contributions by charities.

by the recent debate about the Obama administration's proposal of capping the level of the subsidy for high-income households.

In the absence of tax cheating, this public finance objective yields a simple rule for assessing the optimality of the subsidy rate. The government's program is the following:

$$\text{Max}_\tau \ W = g - \tau g$$

where τ is the subsidy rate and g is the aggregate level of private charitable contributions in the economy. Then, it follows that:

$$\frac{dW}{d\tau} = -g - (1-\tau)\frac{\partial g}{\partial(1-\tau)} = -g(1+\varepsilon_g)$$

where $\varepsilon_g = \frac{dg}{d(1-\tau)}\frac{1-\tau}{g}$ is the elasticity of contributions with respect to $1-\tau$. ε_g is therefore sufficient to infer tax policy, and optimality is determined by the famous *unit elasticity rule* popularized by Feldstein and Clotfelter (1976): The subsidy should be increased if $|\varepsilon_g| \geq 1$.

The simplicity of this rule and the fact that it states that the elasticity of reported contributions is the only statistic necessary to determine the opportunity of raising the subsidy rate explains why most empirical studies have focused on measuring whether this elasticity was superior or inferior to one in absolute value (Auten, Sieg, and Clotfelter (2002), Bakija and Heim (2011), Clotfelter (1980)).

Introducing tax cheating into this simple framework nevertheless substantially modifies the sufficient statistics to be estimated to assess the opportunity for increasing the subsidy rate. If we assume that reported contributions are a mix of contributions producing externality ("True contributions" g) and contributions that do not produce any externality ("Cheating contributions" g_c), the government objective is now:

$$\text{Max } W = g - \tau g - \tau g_c.$$

This yields:

$$\frac{dW}{d\tau} = -(g+g_c) - (1-\tau)\frac{\partial g}{\partial(1-\tau)} + \tau\frac{\partial g_c}{\partial(1-\tau)}.$$

The criterion for increasing the subsidy rate becomes $|\varepsilon_g| \geq \frac{1}{\alpha} + \frac{\tau}{1-\tau}\frac{1-\alpha}{\alpha}|\varepsilon_{g_c}|$. Or equivalently:

$$|\varepsilon_{g_T}| \geq 1 + \frac{1-\alpha}{1-\tau}|\varepsilon_{g_c}| \tag{4.2}$$

where $g_T = g + g_c$ stands for total reported contributions. $\alpha = \frac{g}{g_T}$ is the share of "true" contributions in total reported contributions. ε_{g_T} is the elasticity of total reported contributions with respect to $1 - \tau$, and ε_{g_c} is the elasticity of cheating contributions with respect to $1 - \tau$. Equation 4.2 clearly states that the unit elasticity rule is no longer valid and that ε_{g_T} is no longer sufficient to infer tax policy. An elasticity of reported contribution greater than one in absolute value does not necessarily mean that the subsidy rate should be increased. One also needs to estimate ε_{g_c} and α. If $|\varepsilon_{g_c}|$ is large, or if the share $(1 - \alpha)$ of contributions not producing any externality is large, then focusing only on the elasticity of reported contributions can lead to substantial deviations from the optimal level of the subsidy. The intuition is straightforward. The larger the share of "cheating" contributions $(1 - \alpha)$, the greater the reported contributions' elasticity overstates the true social gain of the subsidy. And the larger the elasticity of "cheating" contributions ε_{g_c}, the greater the revenue loss generated by an increase in the tax subsidy on "cheating" contributions.

A MODEL OF OPTIMAL SUBSIDY WITH TAX CHEATING

We now generalize the intuition of the previous subsection to a model of optimal subsidy for charitable contributions in the presence of tax cheating, with warm-glow of giving and crowding-out of private charitable contributions by direct public provision of public goods.

The setup of the model is as follows. There is a continuum of individuals with density $dv(i)$ over i, $i \in I$, I being an index set. There are basically three goods in the economy: private consumption c, earnings z, and a contribution good g. The utility of individuals is increasing in c and decreasing in z, meaning that labor supply is costly. The contribution good g enters positively in the utility function, which means that we allow individuals to derive positive utility from the fact of giving, following the warm-glow model of Andreoni (2006). To model the public good nature of contributions, we assume that the total level of contributions per capita G enters positively into the utility function of each individual. Since the government can contribute directly to the public good, G is the sum of private and public contributions to the public good ($G = G^0 + G^P$, G^0 being direct public provision of public good, and $G^P = \int g dv(i)$ is total private contributions). In addition, we consider each individual atomistic, so that G is considered as given by each individual to avoid results such as those found in Warr (1982). Finally, we take into account the possibility that individuals evade taxes through the contribution good:[11] individuals can report "cheating contributions" in their tax form and gain an extra subsidy on these cheating contributions. But cheating has a utility cost for individuals, reflecting the probability of being caught and getting a fine, or simply reflecting pro-social compliance preferences. This utility cost makes our evasion model formally comparable to a Allingham and Sandmo (1972) tax evasion model or a Slemrod-type avoidance model (Slemrod and Stephan (2007)).

The individual's program can therefore be summarized as follows:

$$\text{Max}_{c,z,g,g^c} U^i = u^i(c, z, g, g^c, G)$$
$$\text{s.t.} \quad c + g + g_c \leq R + (1-t)z + \tau g + \tau g^c$$

where τ is the tax subsidy rate on contributions and t is the (linear) tax rate on earnings. Note that contrary to the actual US tax system, which works as a deduction of private contributions from taxable income, we do not link t and τ in our model, and formally consider a subsidy working as a tax credit. For a discussion of the optimality of a tax credit over a deduction from taxable income, see Atkinson (1983) or Saez (2004). We denote by $v^i(1-t, 1-\tau, G, R)$ the indirect utility function of individual i. Demand functions, given the tax parameters, are denoted by $z^i(1-t, 1-\tau, G, R)$ for earnings, $g^i(1-t, 1-\tau, G, R)$ for true contributions, and $g^{c^i}(1-t, 1-\tau, G, R)$ for cheating contributions.[12] With the Roy's identity conditions, we can also compute the welfare effect of changes in t and τ for each individual: $v^i_{1-t} = z^i v^i_R$ and $v^i_{1-\tau} = -(g + g^c) v^i_R$.

We make two assumptions regarding the government's program. First we assume that the government can contribute directly to the public good through direct provision financed by tax revenue.[13] The total amount of public contribution to the public good is G^0. Following Saez (2004), we introduce the useful notations $\bar{G} = \bar{G}((1-t, 1-\tau, G^0, R)$, $\bar{G^c} = \bar{G^c}((1-t, 1-\tau, G^0, R)$ and $\bar{Z} = \bar{Z}((1-t, 1-\tau, G^0, R)$ which denote

[11] We consider here only the case where reported contributions and real contributions differ because of tax cheating, but our model easily generalizes to other cases where reported contributions and true contributions differ, as for instance because of underreporting of contributions.

[12] We do not impose any restrictions on the utility function in this model. Note, however, that in the presence of complementarity between true and cheating contributions (g and g_c), any tax enforcement reform aimed at reducing cheating contributions may reduce true contributions as well, which would complicate the choice of the tax enforcement regime that is here taken as given.

[13] In some cases, this assumption may not hold, as is the case for religious organizations in the United States for instance.

average contribution, average cheating contribution and average earning for a given level of public provision of the public good. $\bar{G}_{G0}$ is the crowding-out of public provision on private contributions. We make the assumption that there is no crowding-out on cheating contributions ($\bar{G^c}_{G0} = 0$). Second, we make the assumption that the government can observe $\bar{G}$ at the aggregate level (for instance, through accounting of the nonprofit sector), it is only at the individual level that the government cannot disentangle true from cheating contributions. The government's program thus can be written as follows:

$$\begin{aligned} \text{Max}_{t,\tau,G^0} W &= \int \mu^i v^i (1-t, 1-\tau, G, R) \\ \text{s.t.} \quad t\bar{Z} &\geq R + \tau\bar{G} + \tau\bar{G^c} + G^0 \\ G^0 &\geq 0 \end{aligned}$$

where μ^i is the social weight associated with individual i in the social welfare function. We denote by λ the Lagrange multiplier of the government budget constraint, which is therefore equal to the social marginal value of public funds. The first-order conditions of the government's program are:

$$\begin{cases} \int \mu^i \left[v^i_{1-t} + v^i_G \bar{G}_{1-t} \right] dv(i) + \lambda \left[-\bar{Z} + t\bar{Z}_{1-t} - \tau \left(\bar{G}_{1-t} + \bar{G}^c_{1-t} \right) \right] = 0 \\ \int \mu^i \left[v^i_{1-\tau} + v^i_G \bar{G}_{1-\tau} \right] dv(i) + \lambda \left[t\bar{Z}_{1-\tau} + \bar{G} + \bar{G}^c - \tau \left(\bar{G}_{1-\tau} + \bar{G}^c_{1-\tau} \right) \right] = 0 \\ \int \mu^i \left[v^i_R + v^i_G \bar{G}_R \right] dv(i) + \lambda \left[t\bar{Z}_R - 1 - \tau \left(\bar{G}_R + \bar{G}^c_R \right) \right] = 0 \\ \int \mu^i \left[v^i_G + v^i_G \bar{G}_{G0} \right] dv(i) + \lambda \left[-1 + t\bar{Z}_{G0} - \tau\bar{G}_{G0} \right] = 0 \end{cases}$$

To derive our optimal subsidy formula, we make important additional assumptions. First, we assume that earnings are not affected by G and τ. This assumption is implicitly done in all empirical studies that attempt to measure the elasticity of reported contributions with respect to $1-\tau$. Indeed, it is very likely that people do not change their labor supply because of changes in the subsidy rate on charitable contributions. Still, for public goods such as poverty relief, it may be that increasing the level of the public good provided reduces the labor supply of low-income households. In the absence of clear-cut empirical evidence regarding these types of effects, it seems reasonable to assume zero effect.

Second, we assume that a compensated change on the tax rate on earnings has no effect on contributions. This assumption is also usually made in empirical studies on the elasticity of reported contributions.

This means that a change in the tax rate on earnings only affects charitable contributions to the extent that it affects disposable earnings. Finally, we assume that there are no income effects on earnings at the individual level: $\partial z/\partial R = 0$. Since giving is highly concentrated among high-income households and given that most empirical studies find small-income effects relative to substitution effects for high-ability individuals, it is reasonable to assume that the labor supply of our population of interest is not affected by changes in the lump sum transfer R.

The derivation of our optimal subsidy formula can then be obtained by direct manipulation of the first-order conditions using the previous assumptions. Here, we give a more intuitive proof following the methodology of Roberts (1987) or Saez (2004). We suppose that the government increases the subsidy rate $d\tau > 0$ with an adjustment of public provision such that $d\bar{G} + dG^0 = 0$, thus leaving the size of the external effect unchanged. This change in the subsidy rate τ has four effects:

1. First, it has a mechanical effect on tax revenue: Increasing the subsidy rate on contributions reduces tax revenues by the amount of total private charitable contributions plus total cheating contributions.

$$A = -(\bar{G} + \bar{G^c})d\tau.$$

2. There is also a welfare gain for individuals because of the increase in the subsidy rate. For each individual i, this effect can be written using Roy's identity conditions: $du^i = -v^i_{1-\tau}d\tau = +(g + g^c)v^i_R d\tau$ We introduce the useful notation $\beta(\bar{G}^T) = \int \frac{\mu^i(g+g^c)v^i_R}{\lambda(\bar{G}+\bar{G^c})}d\nu(i)$, which is the average social weight weighted by reported contributions. Integrating over i, we find the aggregate effect on individual's welfare:

$$B = \beta(\bar{G}^T)(\bar{G} + \bar{G^c})d\tau.$$

3. The third effect is due to behavioral responses on contributions. This generates a revenue loss of: $-\tau(d\bar{G} + d\bar{G^c})$. The effect on private contributions can be rewritten using the price effect and the crowding-out effect: $d\bar{G} = -\bar{G}_{1-\tau}d\tau - \bar{G}_{G^0}dG^0 = \frac{-\bar{G}_{1-\tau}d\tau}{1+\bar{G}_{G^0}}$. Assuming no crowding-out on cheating contributions, we can also rewrite $d\bar{G^c} = -\bar{G^c}_{1-\tau}d\tau$. The total effect of behavioral responses on contributions is thus:

$$C = \tau \left(\frac{\bar{G}_{1-\tau} d\tau}{1 + \bar{G}_{G^0}} + \bar{G}^c_{1-\tau} d\tau \right).$$

4. Finally, there is the cost of adjusting the public provision of the public good for the government. By definition, this cost is:

$$D = -dG^0 = d\bar{G}.$$

At the optimum, the sum of these four effects must be zero. $A + B + C + D = 0$. With some manipulations, we therefore get that, at the optimum, the following equation must hold:

$$-\frac{\alpha}{1 + \bar{G}_{G^0}} \varepsilon_g + \frac{\tau(1-\alpha)}{1-\tau} \varepsilon_{g^c} = 1 - \beta\left(\bar{G}^T\right). \tag{4.3}$$

Or equivalently, we can rewrite equation 4.3 with the elasticity of total reported contributions (ε_{g^T}) to make it comparable with equation 4.2:

$$\varepsilon_{g^T} = \left(1 + \bar{G}_{G^0}\right)\left[-\left(1 - \beta\left(\bar{G}^T\right)\right) + (1-\alpha)\left(\frac{1}{1 + \bar{G}_{G^0}} + \frac{\tau}{1-\tau}\right)\varepsilon_{g^c}\right]. \tag{4.4}$$

In the absence of tax cheating, we get that, at the optimum, the following equation must hold:

$$\varepsilon_{g^T} = -\left(1 - \beta\left(\bar{G}^T\right)\right)\left(1 + \bar{G}_{G^0}\right). \tag{4.5}$$

Equation 4.5, which is very similar to the formula derived by Saez (2004), shows that our model generalizes the unit elasticity rule in the absence of tax cheating: With Rawlsian redistributive tastes ($\beta(\bar{G}^T) = 0$) and no crowding-out ($\bar{G}_{G^0} = 0$), equation 4.5 states that at the optimum, we must have $\varepsilon_{g^T} = -1$. In the presence of crowding-out, the absolute value of the elasticity of reported contributions can nevertheless be less than unity.

Equation 4.4 generalizes the insight of the simple public finance formula (4.2) presented in the previous section. In the presence of tax cheating, and with Rawlsian redistributive tastes and no crowding-out, the absolute value of the elasticity of reported contributions must be larger than one at the optimum. Two additional statistics need to be estimated to assess the opportunity of increasing the subsidy rate: α, the share of true contributions in total reported contributions and ε_{g^c} the elasticity of cheating contributions with respect to $1-\tau$. Note also that equation 4.3 can be compared with the sufficient statistics formula derived by Chetty (2009a) in the case of taxable income elasticity with tax sheltering: Taxable income elasticity is no longer sufficient to estimate deadweight loss in this case, and the size of the welfare loss is given by a weighted average of the elasticity of taxable income and of the elasticity of total earnings.

We interpret our results in light of the welfare-sufficient statistics literature by noting that three sufficient statistics are needed to assess the subsidy rate optimality for a given level of tax enforcement. These statistics are the elasticity of reported contributions, the share of "cheating" contributions in total reported contributions, and the elasticity of cheating contributions with respect to $1 - \tau$. Compared with structural approaches, the sufficient statistics approach has two advantages: It allows for fairly general models, such as the welfare model presented here, and it limits the number of parameters to be identified, especially in the case of cheating, whereby identification opportunities are scarce. Of course, the full structural primitives of the model are interesting per se, as for instance the behavioral nonstandard aspects (warm-glow parameters). But to be able to estimate these parameters, it is necessary to impose much more structure on the model. Moreover, estimation of a full structural model in the field of charitable giving is best-suited to randomized experiments in which one can control identification sources, as in DellaVigna, List, and Malmendier, 2009. Here, to the contrary, we claim that important welfare recommendations can be derived by pinning down a few parameters that can be estimated in non-randomized experimental settings. Of course, this is conditional on a certain number of assumptions usually made in the sufficient statistics literature. We rely noticeably on the assumption that the elasticities are somehow immutable parameters, or at least, that they do not vary with small changes of τ. For a discussion of the pros and cons of the welfare-sufficient statistics approach, a thorough analysis is given by Chetty (2009b).

In the remainder of the chapter, we empirically estimate the share of "cheating" contributions, using a natural experiment from the US. We then use our estimates to calibrate our model and provide suggestive evidence that ignoring cheating parameters is likely to lead to large deviations from the optimal subsidy for several credible values of the elasticity of cheating contributions. The source of this discrepancy is first, the share of cheating contributions, which is substantial in most tax systems—especially when marginal tax rates are high—and, second, the price elasticity of cheating contributions, which is likely to be large, especially when tax enforcement is limited, for example when receipts are not required to be attached to the tax return, as is still the case for most contributions in the United States.

4.3.2 *A Natural Experiment on Tax Enforcement*

In this section, we focus on a natural experiment on tax enforcement in the US. The Tax Reform Act of 1969 (TRA69) tightened significantly the rules applying to the functioning of private foundations in order to prevent financial abuses in charitable contributions to private foundations that had been abundantly reported during the 1950s and 1960s.

Several approaches have been taken in prior empirical literature to measure tax evasion. The first approach relies on audited returns. A number of studies therefore utilize cross-sectional variation across taxpayers in observed levels of compliance using the Taxpayer Compliance Monitoring Project (TCMP), which describes the outcome of IRS audits of randomly chosen tax returns. Clotfelter (1983), using TCMP microdata, finds that noncompliance is strongly positively related to the marginal tax rate, whereas Feinstein (1991) finds a negative impact. Klepper and Nagin (1989) show that, across line items, noncompliance rates are related to proxies for the traceability and ambiguity of items. Slemrod (2006) uses TCMP data to investigate specifically the extent of tax evasion through charitable deduction.[14] As with any cross-sectional study of the impact of taxes on behavior, this type of approach is made difficult by the fact that the marginal tax rate is a function of income, making it difficult to identify the tax rate and income effects separately without making strong functional form assumptions. Moreover, the use of audited returns raises issues. If, audited returns come from selected samples of audited taxpayers, then selection becomes a problem. If, on the other hand, audited returns come from random audits, the overall level of evasion is difficult to infer because of the likely strong concentration of cheating behaviors across taxpayers.

A second approach taken in the literature uses experimental methods to investigate tax compliance and its response to tax rates and enforcement. Blumenthal et al. (1998) analyze the results of a randomized controlled experiment conducted by the State of Minnesota Department of Revenue. Kleven et al. (2011) use a randomized experiment in Denmark and find a high level of compliance. Their results also suggest that the informational framework may be even more important than socioeconomic variables in explaining tax compliance.

The third type of approach is indirect and involves observing quantities, such as national income and product accounts from external sources and inferring evasion from these quantities. Gorodnichenko,

[14] Turk et al. (2007) more recently provide evidence on overstatement of charitable contributions using IRS audit data.

Martinez-Vazquez, and Sabirianova Peter (2009), for instance, rely on the gap between consumption in household expenditure surveys and reported earnings before and after a flat tax reform in Russia. The main drawback of this type of approach is that external surveys may lack reliability, and the gap between tax data and survey data is usually very noisy. In a similar vein, a number of studies have focused on indirect sources of identification of evasion. Fisman and Wei (2004) examine the misclassification of Chinese imports from Hong Kong. They find that the gap at the detailed good level between reported Chinese imports from Hong Kong and reported exports from Hong Kong to China is largest for goods with high tax and tariff rates. Hsieh and Moretti (2006) uncover evidence of underpricing and bribes in Iraq's Oil-for-food program by comparing prices charged by Iraq for oil with prices of close substitutes sold on the world market.

Here, we rely on another type of approach by exploiting a natural experiment on tax enforcement with tax data. The approach most closely related to ours is that of Marion and Muehlegger (2008), who examine the effects of a federal regulatory innovation implemented in October 1993, the addition of red dye to untaxed diesel fuel at the point of distribution that significantly lowered the cost of regulatory enforcement. LaLumia and Sallee (2001) also use an enforcement reform that made it very difficult for taxpayers to inappropriately claim additional dependents for tax purpose in order to infer the proportion of tax cheaters. Compared with these papers, our natural experiment focuses specifically on a tightening of the rules for the tax treatment of charities, and allows us to analyze how this change in tax enforcement affected the amount charitable gifts declared for tax purposes.

UNITED STATES, 1969: TIGHTENING OF THE RULES REGULATING PRIVATE FOUNDATIONS

The natural experiment that we focus on took place in the United States in 1969 and significantly modified the tax enforcement of contributions to private foundations.

As shown in figure 4.1, reported charitable contributions of the top 0.01% of US taxpayers experienced a tremendous surge during the 1940s and 1950s. At that time, marginal tax rates for these taxpayers reached an historical peak, with rates as high as 90%. These very high marginal tax rates constituted a major incentive to donate to charitable causes. But these very high tax rates also constituted a significant incentive to engage in tax avoidance behaviors. Indeed, during the 1940s and 1950s, the number of private foundations created surged. Foundations experienced very lax control before 1969, and apart from their tax-exempt status, the rules regulating their functioning were nearly nonexistent. Moreover, the audit rates of foundations by the IRS were very low.[15] Therefore, family charitable trusts and private foundations constituted a highly practical vehicle for tax sheltering.[16] Soon, a large number of abuses were reported.

These abuses are in fact well documented thanks to a series of reports commissioned by different committees appointed by the US Congress or by the US Department of the Treasury. The Cox Committee Report (1952), the Reece Report (1954), the US Treasury Department report (1965), and the Peterson Report (1970) all provide numerous detailed accounts of frauds and abuses. Overall, the most common fraudulent practices included:

- "Self dealing": prior to TRA69, the tax law permitted transactions between a donor or those related to him and his private foundation if they were at *reasonable* or *arm's length* terms. This permitted a variety of doubtful transactions to occur. An anonymous survey of accountants of nearly 500 foundations by Arthur Andersen on behalf of the Peterson Commission reported that 9% of accountants acknowledged common financial self dealing practices within private foundations and that 8% acknowledged that the grants distributed by the foundation were made based on friendship.
- Overvaluation of property contributed to one's own private foundation to increase the amount of one's tax deduction. These types of overvaluation were especially numerous with property for which there was no ascertainable market price.
- Falsely claimed deductions.
- Foundations set up to maintain ownership of a business while benefiting from tax exemption of income generated.
- Political briberies: a famous example involved the Wolfson Foundation that made a long-term agreement for sizable annual payments to Associate Justice Abe Fortas of the US Supreme Court.

Overall, this resulted in extremely low payout rates for a significant number of private foundations that functioned, for many of them, as

[15] Peterson (1970).

[16] It is interesting to note that tax evasion motives have always played a key role in the history of *trusts*. For instance, *trusts* have historically developed for tax evasion reasons in feudal England, as mentioned by North, Wallis, and Weingast (2009). Land trusts were a way of evading the feudal obligations (military service and taxes) linked to land holding by transferring the title of land ownership to a third party (the trustee).

pure tax shelters. Because of growing public concerns, in 1969 the US Congress passed a tax reform act, TRA69, to better regulate the use of private foundations by high-income taxpayers. The provisions of the new tax law included:

- Prohibition of "self dealing," defined as activities that benefit foundation managers, officers, substantial contributors, and other foundation insiders.
- Stricter tax rules on unrelated business income (UBI). In particular, business income that was not closely related to the charitable activities of the organization became subject to tax.
- Establishment of a minimum payout rate as a percentage of investment assets. It was to be the greater of the foundation's actual investment income and a predetermined rate, originally set at 6%. Foundations that failed to meet these requirements were subject to an additional tax.
- Creation of an excise tax on the investment income of private foundations, with an original rate of 4%.
- Further, while the income ceiling of deductions for public charitable foundations was increased from 30% to 50%, it stayed at 20% for private non-operating foundations, with no possibility for carryover.

TRA69 therefore represents an interesting natural experiment on tax enforcement. First, it substantially increased the cost of tax avoiding contributions that became much more difficult to carry on. In addition, the IRS committed to significantly increase the audit rates on foundations. Second, it is important to note that the reform did not affect the price of "true" contributions. The mandatory payout rate was set at a very low level in order to not penalize properly operating foundations, and almost no donors hit the ceiling of 20% prior to the reform. Therefore the reform is expected to have reduced so-called cheating contributions in the model section, without affecting "true" contributions. This gives us an opportunity to estimate a lower bound on the share of contributions that were "cheated" $(1 - \alpha)$.

DATA AND STRATEGY

The effects of TRA69 are visible in figure 4.5, which displays the number of foundations created and terminated from 1960 to 1972. While the number of new foundations was stable around 1,300 every year before 1969, it suddenly dropped to fewer than 300 after 1969. In the meantime, the number of foundations terminated surged. This

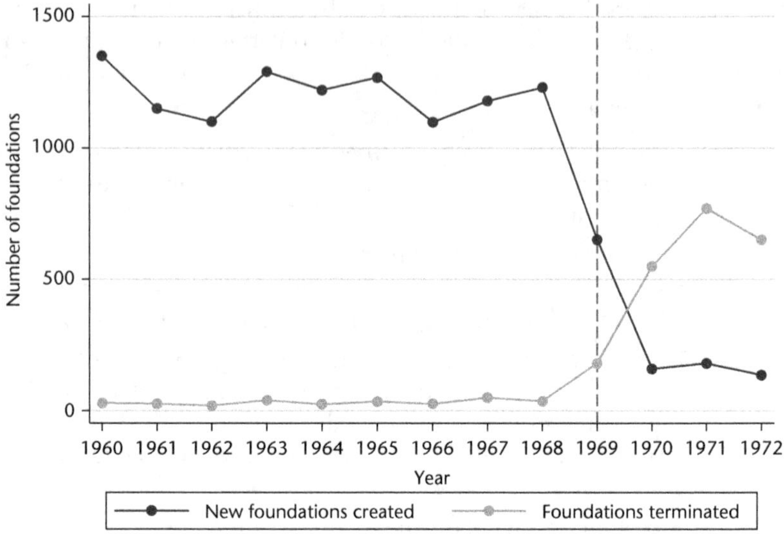

Figure 4.5 Number of New Foundations Created and Foundations Terminated, United States, 1960–1972

Sources: Caplin and Drysdale and the Foundation Center. Reproduced from Research Papers sponsored by the the Commission on Private Philanthropy and Public Needs, volume 3, p. 1638, figure B-13.

evidence suggests that before 1969, a significant number of foundations had been created for tax sheltering purposes. The overall effect of the 1969 tax reform can also be seen in figure 4.6, which shows the percentage of total contributions going to different sectors from 1940 to 1974. Contributions to private foundations are included in the *"All other"* category, whose contributions suddenly dropped from 11% of total giving to 6% of total giving between 1970 and 1974.

To identify the effect of TRA69 on private contributions, we use data from IRS microfiles, with oversampling of high-income taxpayers spanning 1960 to 1990. These samples are repeated cross-sections drawn from individuals' tax returns and contain detailed information on sources of income and deductions claimed.[17] The identification strategy relies on the fact that only a small fraction of taxpayers have their own private foundations. As shown in figure 4.7, households with income below the 99th percentile do not have private foundations. It is

[17] Note that for 1960 to 1972, information on charitable contributions is only present once every two years (in 1960, 1962, 1964, etc.). Note as well that, unfortunately, it is not possible to disentangle contributions by recipient type in these microfiles.

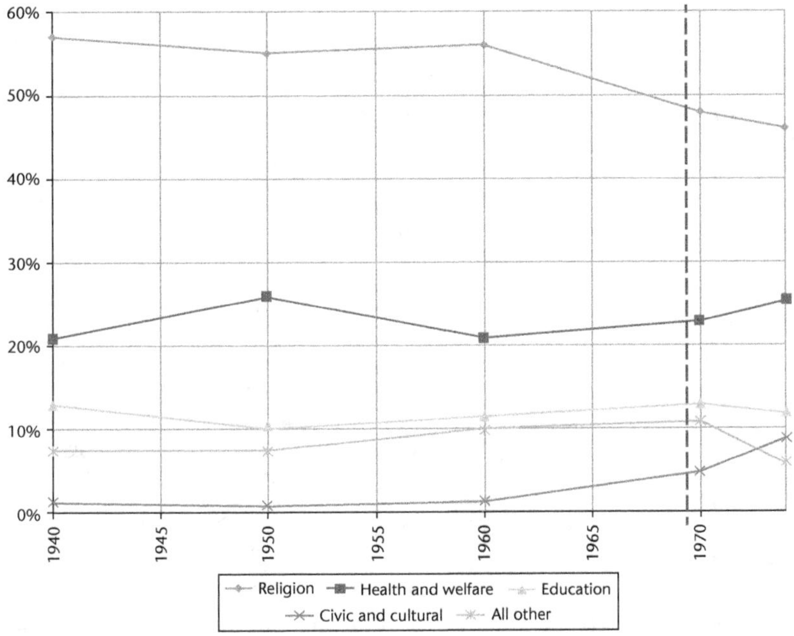

Figure 4.6 Percentage of Total Contributions Going to Each Recipient Area, United States, 1940–1974

Sources: Reproduced from *Report of the Commission on Private Philanthropy and Public Needs*, p. 74.

Notes: "All other": mainly including contributions to private foundations.

only among the top 0.01% of taxpayers that private foundations are a common practice. Substantial evidence also confirms that among these high-income taxpayers (top 0.01%), the majority of reported charitable contributions are made through family trusts and foundations.[18] We therefore use a standard difference-in-difference strategy and look at the effect of the reform on contributions reported by the top 0.01%

[18] A survey conducted in 1970 by the University of Michigan on behalf of the Commission on Private Philanthropy and Public Needs using data from the IRS indicated that nearly 70% of contributions from taxpayers with income above $1,000,000 were dedicated to a remainder category mainly including contributions to foundations. This evidence is also confirmed by recent surveys conducted by the Center on Philanthropy at Indiana University for the Bank of America on high-net-worth households (see Center on Philanthropy (2009)). These surveys demonstrate that most contributions by the very wealthy are donated to their own giving vehicle (trust or private foundation). Interestingly, when asked why they chose to establish a private foundation, the top two answers given by wealthy households in 2008 is "to maximize charitable deductions" (59%) and "to avoid capital gain taxation" (35.7%).

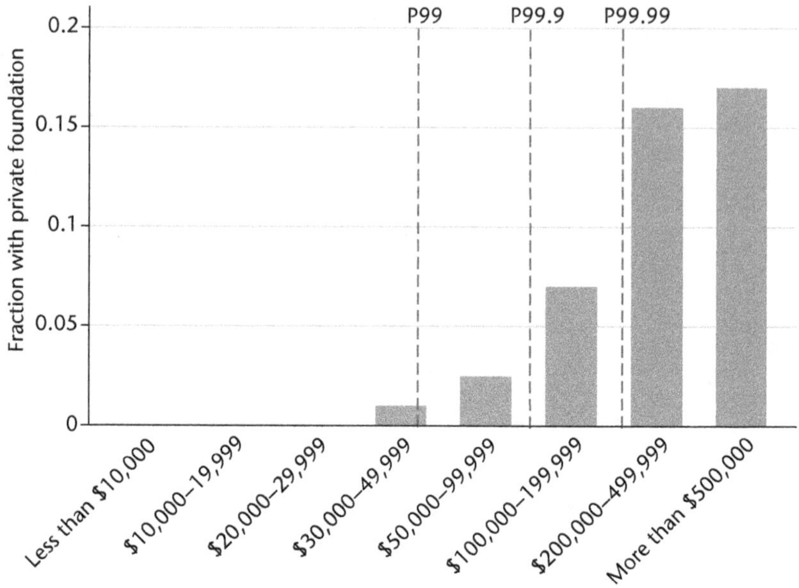

Figure 4.7 Percentage of Households with Charitable Trust or Charitable Foundation by Income Level, United States, 1973

Sources: IRS & Institute for Social Research (Univ. of Michigan). Research Papers, Commission on Private Philanthropy and Public Needs, vol. I, p. 188, Figure 6.

Notes: P99 = 99th percentile of income excluding capital gains.

of taxpayers relative to contributions of other top income groups not rich enough to set up their own private foundations. Figure 4.8 gives graphical evidence of the reform's impact following our identification strategy: It displays the evolution of total reported charitable contributions for the top 0.01% of taxpayers (treated group) and for two income groups unaffected by the reform (control), the top 8% to top 7% of taxpayers (P92–93) and the top 5% to top 4% of taxpayers (P95–96). While the aggregate levels of reported contributions for these three groups exhibit parallel trends during the 1960s, a substantial drop in total contributions appears following TRA69 for the top 0.01% of taxpayers relative to the two unaffected groups, which continue to exhibit the same parallel trends as before TRA69.

Since all relevant information concerning treatment and control in this natural experimental setting comes at the income group level, we collapsed our observations at the income group level to avoid inference issues due to potential correlation of errors within income groups (as is well known since Moulton (1990)). Our standard

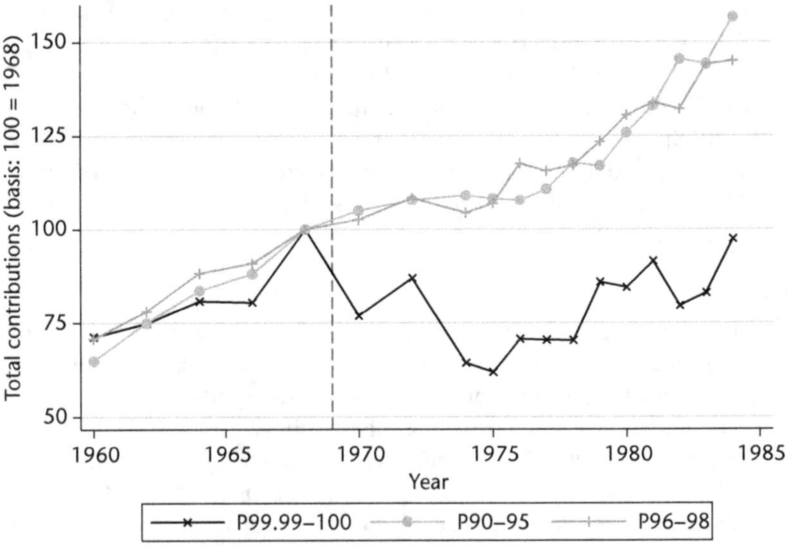

Figure 4.8 Total Contributions by Income Group, United States, 1960–1980

Notes: P99.99–100 = households with income above the 99.99th percentile of income excluding capital gains. P95–96 = households with income above the 95th percentile but below the 96th percentile of income excluding capital gains. P92–93 = households with income above the 92nd percentile but below the 93rd percentile of income excluding capital gains.

difference-in-difference specification to estimate the impact of TRA69 on cheating contributions can thus be summarized as follows:

$$log(contribution)_{i,t} = \sum_i \delta_i + \sum_t \theta_t - (1-\alpha) * \quad (4.6)$$
$$(\text{Treated group} * \text{after } 69) + X_{i,t}\beta + \varepsilon_{i,t}$$

where δ_i are income groups' fixed effects, θ_t are year fixed effects, and $X_{i,t}$ is a vector of controls including percentage of married couples, log of average disposable income, and log of average price to control for possible small variations of price or income across groups. The coefficient before (Treated group $*$ after 69) gives us the percentage drop in total reported contributions for the treatment group that we interpret as $-(1-\alpha)$, the share of contributions that was cheated by the treatment group. Of course, some cheating may still be occurring, even after the 1969 reform, among the treatment group. Our estimates must therefore be interpreted as a lower bound on $1-\alpha$ for very rich taxpayers.

The baseline specification compares group P99.99–100 (top 0.01% of taxpayers) versus group P90–95 (top 10% to top 5% of taxpayers) for the time window 1960 to 1980.[19] We compare 1960 to 1968 with 1970 to 1980.[20] Concerning the timing of the reform, even though some elements of the reform were discussed publicly as early as 1965, it is unlikely that the wealthiest taxpayers had the opportunity to fully anticipate TRA69, because Congressmen moved more quickly than anticipated, and TRA69 was signed by President Nixon on December 30, 1969 before the Peterson Commission had time to release its final report (August 1970).[21]

RESULTS

Results are presented in table 4.3. To control for inference issues arising in difference-in-difference estimates from potential serial correlation of errors by income group (Bertrand, Duflo, and Mullainathan (2004)), cluster-robust standard errors are displayed (with clustering at the income group level). Our baseline estimates (column (2)) state that contributions by the top 0.01% of taxpayers dropped by 28% following TRA69, relative to contributions of income groups not affected by the reform. This suggests that a substantial share of contributions by the very wealthy had been motivated by tax avoidance purposes.

We also present in table 4.3 results controlling for potential bias arising in difference-in-difference analysis due to preexisting trends, as highlighted, for instance, in Wolfers (2006). We first regress our dependent variable (log of contributions) for years prior to the 1969 reform on the same set of regressors, and we include differential time trends across groups.

$$log(contribution)_{i,t} = \sum_i \delta_i + \sum_t \theta_t + \sum_i \eta_i(\delta_i * t) + X_{i,t}\beta + \varepsilon_{i,t}.$$

Then we regress the difference between actual contributions and fitted values of the preceding model for years after the reform on a set of year dummies and an indicator for treatment:

$$log(contribution)_{i,t} - log(\widehat{contribution})_{i,t} = \sum_t \theta_t - (1-\alpha) * (\text{Treated}) + \varepsilon_{i,t}.$$

[19] We also considered a narrower time window (1964 to 1975) in our sensitivity analysis without any loss of robustness.

[20] Note that, unfortunately, information on charitable deductions is not present in the 1969 sample from the IRS.

[21] The US Treasury Report on Private Foundations of 1965 had already asked for the US government to intervene in the actions of foundations and force them to become more accountable through a series of tax laws that would assure the tax-exempt status of foundations would no longer be abused. The recommendations published in the US Department of the Treasury's report included many of the main provisions of TRA69.

Results are presented in column (4) and confirm that the inclusion of controls for preexisting trends does not affect the robustness of the previous estimates. Note that we conducted the same procedure without year 1968 to control for possible shifting behaviors in anticipation of TRA69, and we also conducted the procedure with second-order polynomial trends with no loss of robustness.

The last two columns of table 4.3 present results from placebo regressions, in order to ensure that the estimates are not purely spurious correlations. The first placebo regression consists in comparing two control groups, artificially attributing treatment to group P90–95 after 1969. The second placebo regression consists in comparing the treatment group and the baseline control group before the reform, artificially attributing treatment years to 1965 to 1968. In these two cases, columns (5) and (6) demonstrate that the coefficient on the interaction term *(treated*after reform)* is not significantly different from 0.

Results therefore suggest that a very significant fraction (around 25% to 30%) of contributions reported by the very wealthy before 1969 were driven by tax avoidance or tax cheating purposes. These results have interesting implications for policies regarding tax expenditures. They tend to confirm that higher marginal tax rates reduce importantly voluntary compliance, as noted in some previous studies about evasion (such as, for instance, Clotfelter, 1983 or Poterba, 1987). When marginal tax rates reach very high levels, as was observed from the 1940s to 1960s, tax expenditures are widely utilized as channels of evasion, and tax enforcement likely needs to be increased. Our results using TRA69 as a natural experiment on tax enforcement give a good sense of how significant avoidance strategies can be when marginal tax rates increase.[22] Nevertheless, because of the setting of this natural experiment, only "treatment on the treated" effect can be estimated, and we cannot investigate heterogeneity issues. We have reasons to believe, though, that the propensity to cheat is not likely to be the same across taxpayers, either for idiosyncratic reasons or because of differential incentives to cheat. In particular, the share of contributions that is cheated is clearly a function of marginal tax rates, but in our setting, we are compelled to estimate the share of cheating contributions taking marginal tax rates as given. The inability to estimate the elasticity of cheating contributions with respect to marginal tax rates in the TRA69 case is due to the lack of marginal tax rate variations among

[22] It is worth mentioning, however, that even though top marginal tax rates have substantially decreased and tax enforcement on contributions has been tightened, tax avoidance and evasion through charitable contributions may still be important among the wealthiest taxpayers, as highlighted by Yermack (2008).

Table 4.3 DiD Estimates of the Effect of TRA69 on Charitable Contributions of Top Income Households. Dependent Variable Log of Contributions

	(1) P99.99–100 vs. P90–95	(2) P99.99–100 vs. P90–95	(3) P99.99–100 vs. P80–95	(4) P99.99–100 vs. P90–95	(5) P90–95 vs. P70–90 (*placebo*)	(6) P99.99–100 vs. P90–95 (*placebo*)
Treated*after69	−0.388***	−0.282***	−0.259**	−0.308***		
	(0.0128)	(0.0226)	(0.0474)	(0.0111)		
placebo1					0.0730	
					(0.0494)	
placebo2						−0.0122
						(0.0312)
Controls for income & price	NO	YES	YES	YES	YES	YES
Controls for preexisting trend	NO	NO	NO	YES	NO	NO
N	84	84	98	54	126	30
Number of clusters	6	6	7	6	7	6

Cluster-robust standard errors in parentheses (clustering at the income group level)
* $p < 0.05$, ** $p < 0.01$, *** $p < 0.001$
Placebo 1: Treated group is supposed to be P90–95 and control is P70–90.
Placebo 2: Reform is assumed to be happening in 1964 (1960 to 1964 vs. 1965 to 1968).

the treatment group (top 0.01%) in which every taxpayer hits the top marginal tax rate of the tax schedule. We can nevertheless calibrate our model and show that even for moderate levels of elasticity of "cheating" contributions, one needs an elasticity of reported contribution much larger than one in absolute value in order to justify the existence of tax deductions for charitable giving.

CALIBRATION

Table 4.4 shows the results of the calibrations of our model. The first line of table 4.4 recalls the baseline elasticity rule: when all reported contributions are true contributions and without any crowding-out, tax deductions are justified as long as the elasticity of reported contributions is at least equal to 1 in absolute value. The last panel of the table also shows that with an elasticity of reported charitable

Table 4.4 Calibrations of the Model

Share of true contributions (α)	Deduction rate (τ)	Level of crowding-out ($\bar{G}_{G^0}$)	Elasticity of "cheating" contributions (ε_{g^c})	Elasticity of reported contributions that would justify the subsidy (ε_{g^T})
1	0.3	0	–	1.0
0.75	0.3	0	0.5	1.2
0.75	0.3	0	1	1.4
0.75	0.3	0	1.5	1.5
0.75	0.3	0	2	1.7
0.75	0.5	0	0.5	1.3
0.75	0.5	0	1	1.5
0.75	0.5	0	1.5	1.8
0.75	0.5	0	2	2.0
0.75	0.7	0	0.5	1.4
0.75	0.7	0	1	1.8
0.75	0.7	0	1.5	2.3
0.75	0.7	0	2	2.7
1	0.5	–0.4	1	0.6
0.75	0.5	–0.4	0.5	0.9
0.75	0.5	–0.4	1	1.3
0.75	0.5	–0.4	1.5	1.6
0.75	0.5	–0.4	2	1.9

Note: We assume Rawlsian preferences, *i.e.* $\beta(\bar{G}^T) = 0$. A crowding-out level of -0.4 is consistent with the upper bound of the estimate of Hungerman (2005), and would justify tax deductions for charitable contributions for estimated reported elasticities of around 0.6 in absolute value. Note that in the Ralwsian case chosen here, the social planner is simply maximizing revenues and the marginal welfare weight of individuals above the minimum level of utility in the economy is equal to zero. If to the contrary, the social planner gives a non zero welfare weight to individuals further up the distribution of income, the average social weight weighted by reported contributions will be strictly positive ($\beta(\bar{G}^T) > 0$.) As indicated by formula (4.4), with such redistributive preferences, the level of the elasticity of reported contributions that would justify the subsidy will be lower than the level indicated in this table.

contributions equal to 0.6 in absolute value, as previously estimated with our long panel, one needs to assume a crowding-out of at least 40% in order to justify tax deductions. Such level of crowding-out is in the upper bound of the existing estimates on US data (see Hungerman, 2005 and Gruber and Hungerman, 2007). We can finally see from table 4.4 how taking cheating into account modifies the assessment of the optimality of the tax deduction. Taking the lower bound of our estimates on "cheating contributions," we assume in our calibrations that true contributions represent only 75% of the total reported contributions and that the remaining 25% of contributions are the result of non-compliance behaviors. The different panels of table 4.4 show the elasticity of reported contributions that would be needed to justify optimal charitable tax deductions as a function of the elasticity of "cheating" contributions, in the case of Rawlsian preferences and for varying baseline levels of deduction rates.[23] This calibration exercise shows that, even if we assume a level of crowding-out of 40%, as soon as the elasticity of "cheating" contributions increases from 1 to 0.5, it is not optimal anymore to have tax deductions for an elasticity of reported contribution lower or equal to one in absolute value. Estimates on French data indeed suggest that the elasticity of "cheating" contributions might be close to 1.5 – 2 in absolute value (see Fack and Landais (2016)). If "cheating" contributions are very responsive, total reported contributions would also have to be very responsive for tax deductions to remain optimal. This calibration exercise has obvious limitations—in particular, it only allows for a very simple type of tax deductions that apply to all levels of incomes and all gifts. But this simple model clearly shows that in the presence of tax cheating, the unit elasticity rule is not valid anymore for policy recommendations.

Conclusion

This chapter demonstrates that tax cheating is a first-order concern to evaluate the optimal tax subsidy for charitable contributions. First, we derive a general framework to define the optimality of tax subsidies for contributions in the presence of tax cheating. Our results show that three welfare-sufficient statistics are needed to assess the optimality of subsidies for charitable giving: the price elasticity of

[23] We calibrated our model for baseline deduction rates that span between 0.3 and 0.7 to reflect the evolution of marginal reduction rates over the century for top income households.

reported contributions, the share of "cheating" contributions in total reported contributions, and the price elasticity of "cheating" contributions. Then, we provide new estimates on the elasticity of reported contributions. We improve on previous literature by building a long-term dataset of contributions and marginal tax rates for top incomes in the United States since 1917. We then estimate the share of "cheating" contributions using a natural experiment on tax enforcement of gifts to private foundations in the US. Our results also demonstrate that significant cheating behaviors take place through the charitable deduction channel. We show that the share of cheating contributions is substantial in the absence of third-party reporting of contributions.

These results have important policy implications. First, our calibrations show that tax cheating can no longer be neglected in assessing the optimal policy for charitable contributions. Second, the subsidy rate may not be the only relevant policy instrument to deal optimally with contributions by the very wealthy, contrary to recent proposals for reform that tends to focus on capping the subsidy rate. Indeed, despite the 2005 reform of filing requirements of charitable contributions,[24] tax enforcement of private contributions is still considerably lax in the United States compared with other countries, such as France, that switched to a system very close to third-party reporting of contributions. In this context, cheating contributions are likely to remain significant, and third-party reporting might prove more efficient than capping the subsidy rate.

Appendix 4.A: Long-term series on contributions and effective marginal tax rates by income group

This appendix describes the series of contributions and effective marginal tax rates that we have built using tax return data. The US income tax was begun in 1913 and a deduction for charitable contributions was first created in 1917. Starting in 1916, the Internal Revenue Service (IRS) has published detailed statistical tables on tax returns in *Statistics of Income: Individual Income Tax Returns (SOI)* (the tables for 1913 to 1915 were published in the Annual Reports of the Commissioner of Internal Revenue). These annual 1913 to 2005 tables provide information on the number of tax returns, on the amounts reported for each source of income, and on deductions claimed for a large number of income brackets. Starting in 1960, the IRS has constructed large microfiles of tax returns oversampling taxpayers at the top of the income distribution. These microfiles

[24] From 2006 on, contributions must fulfill the following requirements: for cash contributions in excess of $250, the taxpayer must keep a receipt; for noncash contributions of more than $500, the taxpayer must fill out and file IRS Form 8283.

were constructed annually covering the period 1966 to 1999 and are available to the public.[25]

Piketty and Saez (2003) have also used these same data to compute series on the number of tax units, as well as series on the income level and income share of top income groups since 1913 that we have used for our own computations. To our knowledge, no other research has used these data over the long run to study the evolution of charitable contributions. And, more important, the information available in these data has never been exploited to compute long-term series on effective income taxation. These series on effective marginal tax rates by income groups span a century of numerous and important tax reforms and may therefore be used for a variety of historical tax studies.[26]

Following Piketty and Saez (2003), we computed two types of series that treat differently realized capital gains.[27] The first set of series ranks taxpayers according to income fully including capital gains. But because of the volatility and, more important, of the endogeneity of capital gain realization with respect to taxation, it proved useful to build series ranking taxpayers according to income excluding capital gains. Indeed, at the same level of income, taxpayers with different shares of capital gains in total income face different incentives to give because of different marginal tax rates on earned income and on capital gains. The difference between the two marginal tax rates can be substantial, in particular at the very top of the income distribution (top 0.01% of taxpayers). Therefore, series on contributions for taxpayers ranked according to income including capital gains and series ranked by income excluding capital gains are necessary. In the following subsection, we describe in greater detail the re-ranking issues encountered when computing these two types of series.

Contributions

Series on reported contributions displayed in tables 4.A1 and 4.A2 were constructed as follows. For the 1960 to 2004 period, the series were computed directly from the IRS microfiles. The microfiles allow us to easily rank tax returns by income excluding capital gains or by income including full capital gains. We computed charitable contributions as total charitable contributions including carryover from previous years.[28] To compute charitable contributions as a percentage of total income, we computed total gross income following

[25] No microfiles are available for 1961, 1963, and 1965, and the microfiles for 1967, 1969, and 1971 do not include as many tax return variables as the files for the following years. In particular, these files do not include information on itemized deductions claimed. Note that tabulations of deductions broken down by income brackets are not available for these years, nor for 1951, 1955, 1957, and 1959. For these years, only aggregate deductions were reported in *SOI*.

[26] Computations of effective average tax rates are also available from the authors upon request.

[27] For more details on the rationale behind these two types of series, see Piketty and Saez (2003).

[28] We include carryover in our series in order to guarantee homogeneity over time, because for some years, only total contributions (including carryover) are available from *SOI*.

the same definition of total income as in Piketty and Saez (2003). Note that when computing charitable contributions as a percentage of income, we always consider charitable contributions divided by income *re-including capital gains* for the two types of series of taxpayers (i.e. ranked including or excluding capital gains). This is because capital gains have an income effect on contributions, regardless of the marginal tax rate that the taxpayer faces.

For the 1917 to 1960 period, the series were estimated from the published *SOI* tables by linear interpolation according to the following methodology (all computations are available from the authors upon request):[29]

- Published IRS tables rank tax returns by net income (1917 to 1943) or by AGI (1944 and after). These tables use a large number of income brackets (the thresholds P90, P95, P99, P99.5, P99.9, and P99.99 are usually very close to one of the income bracket thresholds), and one can use standard Pareto interpolation techniques in order to estimate the relevant income levels and income thresholds (P90, P95, etc.) of the distribution of net income (1917 to 1943) and AGI (1944 and after). We then use these thresholds to linearly interpolate the sum of total reported contributions above each threshold. This gives us total reported contributions for the top 10% of taxpayers, the top 5% of taxpayers, and so forth ranked by net income (1917 to 1943) or AGI (1944 and after). Total reported contributions for groups P90–95, P95–99, and so forth are obtained by difference. We checked that our estimation technique does not yield large errors due to linear interpolation approximation. We did the same computation mentioned above with *SOI* for years for which we also have microfiles. Overall, errors are negligible. The main reason is the very large number of income brackets in *SOI* tabulations, especially at the top of the income distribution.

  Note that for a number of years, the filing threshold is very high, and fewer than 10% of tax units actually file returns. To correct for this problem of missing returns, we adopted the same rule as that proposed by Piketty and Saez (2003). The principle is that the filing thresholds for singles is substantially lower than the filing threshold for married households. Thus from 1917 forward, it is always the case that more than 10% of single tax units are actually filing returns, although for some years fewer than 10% of married tax units are filing returns. We adjusted for missing married returns using a simple extrapolation method, based on the assumption that marital ratios (i.e. ratios of married tax units to single men not head of household tax units) across income brackets is constant over years.
- The 1917 to 1960 raw series obtained from linear interpolation were corrected in various ways. First, the raw series were adjusted to control for the switch from net income to AGI brackets in 1943 to 1944. We built homogeneous series computed by AGI levels. To do so, we adjusted upward

[29] Note that information on contributions is not available in SOI for 1918 to 1921, 1951, 1955, 1957, 1959, 1961, 1963, 1965, 1967, 1969, and 1971.

the 1917 to 1943 series computed by net income levels. The potential issue here is that taxpayers may experience some re-ranking, because taxpayers deducting large contributions are mechanically ranked higher on an AGI scale than on net income (AGI minus deductions) scale. We were able to check with the IRS microfiles for 1960 to 2004 that re-ranking issues do not affect the series of contributions for income groups below the top 0.1%. For taxpayers ranked above the top 0.1%, slight corrections proved necessary, however, and we used multipliers computed from IRS microfiles to adjust contributions' series of the top 0.1% for 1917 to 1943.

- Next, and most importantly, corrections need to be made to go from AGI series to gross income series (including and excluding capital gains). The tax treatment of capital gains has changed many times since 1913: from 1913 to 1933, 100% of capital gains were included in net income (there was no capital gains exclusion); from 1934 to 1937, 70% of capital gains were included in net income (i.e., 30% of capital gains were excluded); from 1938 to 1941, 60% of capital gains were included in net income (i.e., 40% of capital gains were excluded); from 1942 to 1978, 50% of capital gains were included in net income (1942 to 1943) or in AGI (1944 to 1978) (i.e., 50% of capital gains were excluded); from 1979 to 1986, 40% of capital gains were included in AGI (i.e., 60% of capital gains were excluded); and from 1987 forward, 100% of capital gains were included in AGI (there was, once again, no capital gains exclusion). The main issue when going from AGI to gross income series is re-ranking of taxpayers. This issue is likely to arise if taxpayers with a high share of capital gains contribute differently from taxpayers with a low level of capital gains. A priori, re-ranking effects are totally ambiguous. This is why we relied on microfiles for 1960 to 2004 to compute adjustment coefficients taking advantage of the reforms in capital gains inclusion in AGI. Our analysis suggested that for income groups below the top 0.1%, adjustments are not necessary, because there is no significant difference between the series ranked by AGI, gross income including capital gains, and gross income excluding capital gains. For income groups above the top 0.1%, some adjustments proved necessary, because our analysis showed that taxpayers with large capital gain realizations contribute less for a given level of income, which is in line with the fact that their marginal tax rate is lower *ceteris paribus*. To go from series ranked by AGI to series ranked by gross income fully including capital gains, we therefore had to adjust upward contributions of the P99.9–P99.99 income group and downward contributions of the P99.99–100 income group. Note that these adjustments are always lower than 5% and that for 1913 to 1933, we made no adjustment to compute series fully including capital gains, because AGI did include 100% of capital gains. We followed the same strategy to go from AGI series to series ranked by income excluding capital gains. All adjustment coefficients are available from the authors upon request.

Effective Marginal Tax Rates

To compute series of effective marginal tax rates by top income groups, we relied on different sources. First, we used the "Synopsis of federal tax laws" in *Statistics of Income for 1959*, part I, (pp. 307–43). This synopsis provides all the details of the individual income tax laws for 1913 to 1950. In particular, it gives detailed tables on requirements for filing, exemption levels, credits for dependents, normal tax rates, surtax rates, capital gains taxes, earned income credit, deductions, and so forth. For 1950 to 1960, we relied directly on the information given every year on tax laws in the *SOI*. For the years after 1960, we used NBER's Taxsim9 simulator. Note that we focus on federal income tax and do not compute state income tax in our simulator. Note as well that marginal tax rates are computed at the average income level of the income group. For most income groups, this is not an issue, because there is very little difference between the marginal tax rate at the average income of the group and the average marginal tax rate in the group. For the top 0.01% of taxpayers, though, the difference may matter. Unfortunately, there is no easy way to cope with this issue, due to the lack of microdata before 1960.

For years prior to 1960, the series are computed as follows. We take the average gross income of the income group. We deduct average reported adjustments and deductions that we interpolated following the same strategy as for contributions. With no information on the average matrimonial status of taxpayers by income group, we focus on the case of a married couple filing jointly with two children. Concerning capital gains, we use the composition series in Piketty and Saez (2003), which give the share of capital gains in total income by income groups for series ranked including and excluding capital gains.[30] We then compute income tax liability and marginal income tax rates on earned income and on capital gains.

Among the many features that our 1913 to 1960 Federal Income Tax simulator takes into account, we can mention the alternative tax on capital gains, the Earned Income Credit, as well as all special taxes and refunds, such as the Defense Tax and Victory Tax.

[30] Note, however, that due to data limitations, these capital gains series cannot disentangle short-term from long-term capital gains. Our computations for 1913 to 1960 are therefore based on the assumption that all capital gains are long-term capital gains with respect to the functioning of the alternative tax on capital gains.

Table 4.A1 Contributions as a Percentage of Total Income (Including K Gains) for Top Income Groups in the United States (Fractiles are Defined by Total Income Including Capital Gains)

	P90–100 (1)	P95–100 (2)	P99–100 (3)	P99.5–100 (4)	P99.9–100 (5)	P99.99–100 (6)	P90–95 (7)	P95–99 (8)	P99–99.5 (9)	P99.5–99.9 (10)	P99.9–99.99 (11)
1917		2.00%	2.53%	2.78%	3.47%	4.83%		1.26%	1.50%	1.80%	2.56%
1922	1.62%	1.98%	2.68%	2.79%	3.49%	4.86%	0.64%	1.18%	2.32%	2.06%	2.77%
1923	1.75%	2.16%	2.82%	3.04%	3.86%	5.39%	0.73%	1.42%	2.11%	2.23%	3.09%
1924	1.69%	2.05%	2.61%	2.87%	3.69%	5.19%	0.75%	1.39%	1.74%	2.03%	2.90%
1925	1.57%	1.83%	2.31%	2.49%	3.02%	3.71%	0.75%	1.18%	1.63%	1.89%	2.57%
1926	1.68%	1.97%	2.51%	2.73%	3.29%	4.05%	0.80%	1.23%	1.74%	2.05%	2.79%
1927	1.71%	1.93%	2.56%	2.77%	3.36%	4.19%	0.96%	1.04%	1.77%	2.02%	2.80%
1928	1.64%	1.84%	2.35%	2.50%	2.92%	3.54%	0.91%	1.02%	1.70%	1.88%	2.43%
1929	1.65%	1.85%	2.37%	2.55%	2.97%	3.57%	0.95%	1.02%	1.65%	1.90%	2.46%
1930	1.70%	1.97%	2.79%	3.10%	3.93%	5.23%	0.98%	1.01%	1.78%	2.14%	3.05%
1931	1.67%	1.93%	2.86%	3.19%	4.02%	5.38%	1.06%	1.02%	1.91%	2.31%	3.18%
1932	1.79%	1.98%	3.09%	3.29%	3.97%	5.63%	1.35%	0.97%	2.53%	2.56%	3.14%
1933	1.65%	1.74%	2.59%	2.65%	3.06%	3.94%	1.41%	0.91%	2.40%	2.19%	2.58%
1934	1.49%	1.58%	2.40%	2.57%	3.21%	4.39%	1.21%	0.82%	1.87%	1.94%	2.60%
1935	1.43%	1.57%	2.23%	2.41%	3.04%	4.19%	1.05%	0.86%	1.69%	1.76%	2.44%
1936	1.41%	1.57%	2.12%	2.29%	3.00%	4.50%	0.96%	0.88%	1.54%	1.55%	2.24%
1937	1.55%	1.79%	2.37%	2.61%	3.49%	5.26%	0.91%	1.13%	1.63%	1.73%	2.59%
1938	1.55%	1.78%	2.37%	2.55%	3.11%	3.91%	1.00%	1.18%	1.82%	1.99%	2.64%
1939	1.57%	1.84%	2.45%	2.68%	3.46%	5.04%	0.92%	1.22%	1.78%	1.94%	2.67%
1940	1.59%	1.93%	2.49%	2.72%	3.49%	4.97%	0.75%	1.33%	1.84%	1.98%	2.73%
1941	1.71%	1.87%	2.26%	2.41%	2.99%	4.06%	1.30%	1.43%	1.81%	1.85%	2.45%
1942	1.71%	1.90%	2.23%	2.34%	2.77%	3.38%	1.25%	1.55%	1.89%	1.95%	2.48%
1943	1.74%	1.93%	2.27%	2.40%	2.88%	3.85%	1.27%	1.58%	1.91%	1.98%	2.49%

1944	1.66%	1.95%	2.50%	2.69%	3.31%	4.16%	0.98%	1.42%	1.99%	2.17%	2.93%
1945	1.86%	2.17%	2.77%	2.99%	3.67%	4.56%	1.07%	1.55%	2.20%	2.41%	3.28%
1946	1.81%	2.05%	2.57%	2.79%	3.39%	3.94%	1.17%	1.54%	1.99%	2.29%	3.11%
1947	1.96%	2.23%	2.78%	3.02%	3.69%	4.39%	1.27%	1.72%	2.15%	2.47%	3.34%
1948	1.67%	1.85%	2.49%	2.73%	3.40%	4.32%	1.21%	1.25%	1.83%	2.18%	2.95%
1949	1.82%	2.01%	2.72%	2.99%	3.75%	4.84%	1.35%	1.36%	2.03%	2.35%	3.23%
1950	1.72%	1.87%	2.42%	2.65%	3.24%	4.95%	1.32%	1.32%	1.80%	2.14%	2.58%
1952	1.95%	2.21%	2.96%	3.26%	4.14%	5.41%	1.37%	1.54%	2.19%	2.57%	3.55%
1953	2.04%	2.31%	3.14%	3.47%	4.47%	5.69%	1.47%	1.63%	2.35%	2.70%	3.90%
1954	2.07%	2.36%	3.23%	3.57%	4.57%	6.51%	1.42%	1.61%	2.35%	2.75%	3.58%
1956	2.22%	2.61%	3.45%	3.68%	4.79%	6.98%	1.33%	1.90%	2.86%	2.75%	3.65%
1958	2.58%	2.89%	3.83%	4.14%	5.57%	8.54%	1.92%	2.13%	3.07%	2.99%	4.07%
1960	2.72%	3.10%	3.96%	4.44%	5.78%	8.72%	1.95%	2.41%	2.76%	3.32%	4.12%
1962	2.76%	3.08%	3.97%	4.45%	5.99%	8.62%	2.10%	2.38%	2.79%	3.18%	4.48%
1964	2.71%	3.00%	3.74%	4.20%	5.76%	7.82%	2.09%	2.40%	2.66%	2.88%	4.46%
1966	2.55%	2.82%	3.55%	4.00%	5.38%	7.39%	1.98%	2.24%	2.45%	2.79%	4.15%
1968	2.64%	2.90%	3.71%	4.13%	5.33%	6.62%	2.06%	2.20%	2.59%	2.97%	4.46%
1970	2.60%	2.88%	3.70%	4.19%	5.63%	7.79%	2.05%	2.31%	2.58%	3.05%	4.41%
1972	2.54%	2.87%	3.76%	4.22%	5.68%	7.92%	1.88%	2.20%	2.64%	2.98%	4.32%
1973	2.37%	2.64%	3.47%	3.94%	5.15%	7.07%	1.84%	2.06%	2.43%	3.00%	4.16%
1974	2.35%	2.60%	3.40%	3.80%	4.90%	6.77%	1.85%	2.04%	2.51%	2.96%	4.01%
1975	2.40%	2.68%	3.52%	3.99%	5.23%	7.39%	1.85%	2.11%	2.52%	3.08%	4.16%
1976	2.43%	2.77%	3.62%	4.13%	5.44%	7.61%	1.77%	2.19%	2.51%	3.15%	4.37%
1977	2.38%	2.70%	3.57%	4.04%	5.23%	7.13%	1.75%	2.11%	2.52%	3.13%	4.24%
1978	2.35%	2.63%	3.45%	3.92%	5.24%	7.40%	1.80%	2.07%	2.41%	2.92%	4.21%

(*continued*)

Table 4.A1 Continued

	P90–100 (1)	P95–100 (2)	P99–100 (3)	P99.5–100 (4)	P99.9–100 (5)	P99.99–100 (6)	P90–95 (7)	P95–99 (8)	P99–99.5 (9)	P99.5–99.9 (10)	P99.9–99.99 (11)
1979	2.33%	2.62%	3.27%	3.61%	4.44%	5.24%	1.73%	2.11%	2.43%	2.84%	3.90%
1980	2.41%	2.71%	3.40%	3.72%	4.52%	5.54%	1.81%	2.19%	2.61%	2.98%	3.91%
1981	2.55%	2.86%	3.60%	3.94%	4.71%	5.43%	1.94%	2.28%	2.73%	3.18%	4.26%
1982	2.49%	2.66%	3.20%	3.37%	3.62%	3.81%	2.14%	2.22%	2.71%	3.10%	3.49%
1983	2.54%	2.75%	3.27%	3.40%	3.54%	3.57%	2.06%	2.31%	2.89%	3.23%	3.52%
1984	2.54%	2.75%	3.21%	3.41%	3.30%	3.63%	2.08%	2.34%	2.58%	3.54%	3.05%
1985	2.71%	2.94%	3.54%	3.87%	4.21%	3.76%	2.18%	2.38%	2.48%	3.44%	4.55%
1986	2.75%	3.00%	3.62%	3.87%	4.16%	3.23%	2.09%	2.29%	2.65%	3.46%	4.93%
1987	2.51%	2.72%	3.12%	3.16%	3.53%	4.10%	2.03%	2.35%	3.01%	2.76%	3.17%
1988	2.31%	2.40%	2.57%	2.61%	2.89%	3.65%	2.06%	2.21%	2.43%	2.26%	2.34%
1989	2.42%	2.54%	2.76%	2.86%	3.25%	3.96%	2.12%	2.31%	2.42%	2.40%	2.76%
1990	2.38%	2.49%	2.68%	2.75%	3.07%	3.85%	2.11%	2.28%	2.48%	2.38%	2.54%
1991	2.53%	2.67%	2.96%	3.08%	3.48%	4.25%	2.20%	2.40%	2.60%	2.66%	3.00%
1992	2.44%	2.53%	2.62%	2.69%	2.93%	3.39%	2.23%	2.44%	2.40%	2.41%	2.61%
1993	2.60%	2.75%	3.14%	3.27%	3.77%	4.54%	2.24%	2.38%	2.71%	2.71%	3.25%
1994	2.62%	2.79%	3.25%	3.47%	4.07%	5.25%	2.21%	2.34%	2.57%	2.79%	3.28%
1995	2.52%	2.64%	3.03%	3.19%	3.73%	4.65%	2.21%	2.24%	2.52%	2.55%	3.13%
1996	2.59%	2.73%	3.13%	3.34%	3.96%	4.81%	2.22%	2.28%	2.43%	2.54%	3.34%
1997	2.75%	2.90%	3.32%	3.57%	4.31%	5.33%	2.30%	2.40%	2.41%	2.56%	3.54%
1998	2.70%	2.84%	3.19%	3.35%	3.82%	4.70%	2.27%	2.40%	2.56%	2.68%	3.14%
1999	2.82%	2.96%	3.28%	3.47%	4.00%	4.99%	2.38%	2.53%	2.51%	2.67%	3.24%
2000	2.81%	2.92%	3.26%	3.43%	3.89%	4.84%	2.46%	2.44%	2.52%	2.66%	3.06%
2001	2.85%	2.97%	3.33%	3.54%	4.06%	4.90%	2.50%	2.53%	2.55%	2.82%	3.39%
2002	2.91%	3.01%	3.34%	3.55%	4.05%	4.98%	2.65%	2.64%	2.63%	2.91%	3.36%
2003	2.97%	3.09%	3.44%	3.67%	4.24%	5.26%	2.62%	2.69%	2.62%	2.89%	3.44%
2004	3.00%	3.11%	3.42%	3.61%	4.16%	4.98%	2.68%	2.70%	2.69%	2.79%	3.46%

Note: Authors' computation from Statistics of Income (1917 to 1960) and IRS samples of taxpayers (1962 to 2005).

Source: Contributions are total reported contributions including carry-over from previous years.

P90–100: Taxpayers with income above the 90th percentile of the income distribution including K gains.

P90–95: Taxpayers with income between the 90th and the 95th percentile of the income distribution including K gains.

P95–99: Taxpayers with income between the 95th and the 99th percentile of the income distribution including K gains, etc.

Table 4.A2 Contributions as a Percentage of Total Income (Including K Gains) for Top Income Groups in the United States (Fractiles are Defined by Total Income Including Capital Gains)

	P90–100 (1)	P95–100 (2)	P99–100 (3)	P99.5–100 (4)	P99.9–100 (5)	P99.99–100 (6)	P90–95 (7)	P95–99 (8)	P99–99.5 (9)	P99.5–99.9 (10)	P99.9–99.99 (11)
1917		1.89%	2.34%	2.54%	3.07%	3.87%		1.26%	1.50%	1.80%	2.54%
1922	1.70%	2.10%	2.91%	3.10%	4.13%	6.47%	0.64%	1.18%	2.32%	2.06%	2.98%
1923	1.87%	2.32%	3.15%	3.49%	4.80%	8.35%	0.73%	1.42%	2.11%	2.23%	3.10%
1924	1.79%	2.19%	2.89%	3.25%	4.48%	7.73%	0.75%	1.39%	1.74%	2.03%	2.88%
1925	1.60%	1.89%	2.45%	2.70%	3.47%	5.12%	0.75%	1.18%	1.63%	1.89%	2.55%
1926	1.66%	1.95%	2.51%	2.74%	3.36%	4.38%	0.80%	1.23%	1.74%	2.05%	2.76%
1927	1.68%	1.91%	2.55%	2.78%	3.45%	4.53%	0.96%	1.04%	1.77%	2.02%	2.79%
1928	1.59%	1.80%	2.34%	2.51%	3.00%	3.90%	0.91%	1.02%	1.70%	1.88%	2.41%
1929	1.60%	1.80%	2.35%	2.54%	3.02%	3.85%	0.95%	1.02%	1.65%	1.90%	2.45%
1930	1.69%	1.95%	2.79%	3.10%	3.98%	5.51%	0.98%	1.01%	1.78%	2.14%	3.04%
1931	1.65%	1.90%	2.80%	3.11%	3.90%	5.22%	1.06%	1.02%	1.91%	2.31%	3.12%
1932	1.87%	2.10%	3.34%	3.61%	4.61%	7.44%	1.35%	0.97%	2.53%	2.56%	3.23%
1933	1.82%	1.97%	3.07%	3.29%	4.31%	7.83%	1.41%	0.91%	2.40%	2.19%	2.49%
1934	1.59%	1.73%	2.71%	3.00%	4.08%	6.95%	1.21%	0.82%	1.87%	1.94%	2.68%
1935	1.47%	1.64%	2.39%	2.62%	3.49%	5.50%	1.05%	0.86%	1.69%	1.76%	2.49%
1936	1.47%	1.66%	2.30%	2.53%	3.51%	6.01%	0.96%	0.88%	1.54%	1.55%	2.31%
1937	1.61%	1.88%	2.55%	2.84%	3.97%	6.61%	0.91%	1.13%	1.63%	1.73%	2.70%
1938	1.65%	1.92%	2.67%	2.97%	4.02%	6.62%	1.00%	1.18%	1.82%	1.99%	2.71%
1939	1.71%	2.04%	2.87%	3.25%	4.66%	8.85%	0.92%	1.22%	1.78%	1.94%	2.69%
1940	1.74%	2.16%	2.96%	3.35%	4.85%	9.20%	0.75%	1.33%	1.84%	1.98%	2.79%
1941	1.90%	2.15%	2.82%	3.16%	4.58%	8.58%	1.30%	1.43%	1.81%	1.85%	2.75%
1942	1.94%	2.22%	2.85%	3.18%	4.57%	8.61%	1.25%	1.55%	1.89%	1.95%	2.85%

(continued)

Table 4.A2 Continued

	P90–100 (1)	P95–100 (2)	P99–100 (3)	P99.5–100 (4)	P99.9–100 (5)	P99.99–100 (6)	P90–95 (7)	P95–99 (8)	P99–99.5 (9)	P99.5–99.9 (10)	P99.9–99.99 (11)
1943	1.94%	2.22%	2.85%	3.19%	4.65%	9.59%	1.27%	1.58%	1.91%	1.98%	2.89%
1944	1.86%	2.24%	3.11%	3.54%	5.25%	10.10%	0.98%	1.42%	1.99%	2.17%	3.35%
1945	2.04%	2.43%	3.33%	3.79%	5.59%	10.78%	1.07%	1.55%	2.20%	2.41%	3.73%
1946	1.98%	2.29%	3.10%	3.56%	5.25%	9.68%	1.17%	1.54%	1.99%	2.29%	3.50%
1947	2.12%	2.47%	3.30%	3.77%	5.49%	9.76%	1.27%	1.72%	2.15%	2.47%	3.74%
1948	1.83%	2.08%	2.99%	3.44%	5.08%	9.48%	1.21%	1.25%	1.83%	2.18%	3.32%
1949	1.96%	2.23%	3.20%	3.67%	5.37%	9.77%	1.35%	1.36%	2.03%	2.35%	3.55%
1950	1.85%	2.07%	2.85%	3.26%	4.66%	9.93%	1.32%	1.32%	1.80%	2.14%	2.98%
1954	2.18%	2.54%	3.69%	4.26%	6.37%	12.03%	1.42%	1.61%	2.35%	2.75%	4.09%
1956	2.31%	2.77%	3.87%	4.31%	6.52%	12.67%	1.33%	1.90%	2.86%	2.75%	3.96%
1958	2.65%	3.01%	4.19%	4.69%	7.16%	13.93%	1.92%	2.13%	3.07%	2.99%	4.41%
1960	2.82%	3.26%	4.35%	5.08%	7.31%	13.76%	1.96%	2.45%	2.78%	3.54%	4.54%
1962	2.86%	3.24%	4.38%	5.10%	7.72%	14.00%	2.11%	2.43%	2.85%	3.34%	5.02%
1964	2.82%	3.19%	4.24%	4.87%	7.63%	13.80%	2.08%	2.44%	2.92%	3.01%	4.92%
1966	2.60%	2.91%	3.77%	4.40%	6.40%	11.50%	1.98%	2.26%	2.39%	2.92%	4.18%
1968	2.69%	3.00%	4.00%	4.58%	6.74%	11.88%	2.05%	2.21%	2.65%	2.97%	4.64%
1970	2.64%	2.94%	3.86%	4.45%	6.55%	11.40%	2.07%	2.31%	2.63%	3.05%	4.56%
1972	2.56%	2.91%	3.97%	4.49%	6.50%	10.56%	1.89%	2.18%	2.87%	3.11%	4.76%
1973	2.41%	2.70%	3.65%	4.22%	5.93%	9.71%	1.85%	2.09%	2.48%	3.12%	4.51%
1974	2.38%	2.63%	3.53%	4.00%	5.43%	8.65%	1.89%	2.03%	2.56%	3.05%	4.20%
1975	2.42%	2.73%	3.61%	4.12%	5.60%	8.83%	1.85%	2.17%	2.56%	3.14%	4.30%
1976	2.44%	2.78%	3.70%	4.22%	5.84%	9.09%	1.81%	2.20%	2.62%	3.14%	4.51%
1977	2.39%	2.74%	3.66%	4.17%	5.70%	8.92%	1.75%	2.14%	2.61%	3.14%	4.41%
1978	2.36%	2.66%	3.53%	4.02%	5.62%	8.62%	1.80%	2.10%	2.52%	2.93%	4.43%
1979	2.37%	2.69%	3.47%	3.88%	5.12%	7.10%	1.73%	2.15%	2.54%	2.91%	4.15%

1980	2.47%	2.79%	3.55%	3.94%	5.14%	7.33%	1.86%	2.25%	2.64%	3.02%	4.12%
1981	2.60%	2.95%	3.88%	4.34%	5.62%	7.93%	1.96%	2.30%	2.82%	3.35%	4.56%
1982	2.54%	2.74%	3.36%	3.65%	4.25%	5.34%	2.16%	2.27%	2.62%	3.11%	3.69%
1983	2.59%	2.85%	3.45%	3.70%	4.21%	4.95%	2.07%	2.37%	2.81%	3.24%	3.81%
1984	2.59%	2.82%	3.45%	3.74%	3.90%	5.18%	2.12%	2.32%	2.65%	3.58%	3.18%
1985	2.75%	3.04%	3.81%	4.27%	5.13%	5.18%	2.12%	2.40%	2.55%	3.40%	5.11%
1986	2.87%	3.20%	4.10%	4.59%	4.07%	4.84%	2.09%	2.33%	2.54%	5.09%	3.56%
1987	2.49%	2.71%	3.13%	3.17%	3.54%	4.35%	2.03%	2.35%	2.99%	2.82%	3.09%
1988	2.30%	2.42%	2.59%	2.63%	2.89%	3.67%	2.01%	2.23%	2.44%	2.33%	2.39%
1989	2.40%	2.52%	2.77%	2.88%	3.26%	3.88%	2.10%	2.27%	2.43%	2.47%	2.87%
1990	2.37%	2.48%	2.68%	2.74%	3.06%	3.77%	2.09%	2.29%	2.51%	2.40%	2.63%
1991	2.52%	2.68%	2.98%	3.09%	3.49%	4.21%	2.17%	2.41%	2.65%	2.70%	3.07%
1992	2.42%	2.51%	2.59%	2.66%	2.86%	3.21%	2.21%	2.43%	2.36%	2.43%	2.65%
1993	2.55%	2.71%	3.06%	3.20%	3.60%	4.40%	2.18%	2.37%	2.65%	2.78%	3.13%
1994	2.57%	2.74%	3.17%	3.38%	4.02%	5.11%	2.17%	2.33%	2.56%	2.72%	3.37%
1995	2.49%	2.61%	2.96%	3.12%	3.66%	4.56%	2.21%	2.25%	2.50%	2.55%	3.15%
1996	2.56%	2.70%	3.12%	3.31%	3.93%	5.01%	2.20%	2.25%	2.52%	2.61%	3.26%
1997	2.69%	2.85%	3.27%	3.47%	4.22%	5.56%	2.25%	2.38%	2.57%	2.58%	3.41%
1998	2.64%	2.80%	3.15%	3.34%	3.91%	5.02%	2.16%	2.40%	2.51%	2.63%	3.22%
1999	2.77%	2.91%	3.22%	3.43%	4.03%	5.05%	2.37%	2.52%	2.48%	2.69%	3.38%
2000	2.83%	2.96%	3.30%	3.48%	3.97%	4.84%	2.43%	2.52%	2.60%	2.82%	3.41%
2001	2.87%	3.01%	3.36%	3.56%	4.13%	5.20%	2.49%	2.61%	2.67%	2.89%	3.45%
2002	2.89%	2.99%	3.32%	3.52%	4.09%	5.31%	2.63%	2.64%	2.66%	2.86%	3.34%
2003	2.94%	3.10%	3.42%	3.65%	4.30%	5.53%	2.50%	2.75%	2.67%	2.88%	3.49%
2004	3.00%	3.12%	3.47%	3.65%	4.30%	5.32%	2.65%	2.70%	2.81%	2.82%	3.60%

Note: Authors' computation from Statistics of Income (1917 to 1960) and IRS samples of taxpayers (1962 to 2005).

Source: Contributions are total reported contributions including carry-over from previous years.
P90–100: Taxpayers with income above the 90th percentile of the income distribution excluding K gains.
P90–95: Taxpayers with income between the 90th and the 95th percentile of the income distribution excluding K gains.
P95–99: Taxpayers with income between the 95th and the 99th percentile of the income distribution excluding K gains, etc.

Table 4.A3 Effective Marginal Tax Rates on Earned Income for Top Income Groups in the United States

	Fractiles defined including K gains						Fractiles defined excluding K gains					
	P90–95 (1)	P95–99 (2)	P99–99.5 (3)	P99.5–99.9 (4)	P99.9–99.99 (5)	P99.99–100 (6)	P90–95 (7)	P95–99 (8)	P99–99.5 (9)	P99.5–99.9 (10)	P99.9–99.99 (11)	P99.99–100 (12)
1913	1.0%	1.0%	1.0%	1.0%	2.0%	5.0%	1.0%	1.0%	1.0%	1.0%	2.0%	5.0%
1914	1.0%	1.0%	1.0%	1.0%	2.0%	5.0%	1.0%	1.0%	1.0%	1.0%	2.0%	5.0%
1915	1.0%	1.0%	1.0%	1.0%	3.0%	6.0%	1.0%	1.0%	1.0%	1.0%	2.0%	6.0%
1916	2.0%	2.0%	2.0%	2.0%	4.0%	11.0%	2.0%	2.0%	2.0%	2.0%	4.0%	11.0%
1917	0.0%	2.0%	5.0%	8.0%	16.0%	50.0%	0.0%	2.0%	5.0%	8.0%	16.0%	50.0%
1918	0.0%	6.0%	14.0%	17.0%	33.0%	72.0%	0.0%	6.0%	14.0%	17.0%	34.0%	72.0%
1919	0.0%	4.0%	11.0%	15.0%	33.0%	68.0%	4.0%	4.0%	11.0%	15.0%	33.0%	68.0%
1920	4.0%	4.0%	11.0%	15.0%	29.0%	64.0%	4.0%	4.0%	11.0%	15.0%	30.0%	64.0%
1921	0.0%	4.0%	6.0%	13.0%	25.0%	60.0%	0.0%	4.0%	6.0%	13.0%	26.0%	64.0%
1922	0.0%	4.0%	9.0%	12.0%	26.0%	57.0%	0.0%	4.0%	9.0%	12.0%	27.0%	57.0%
1923	0.0%	3.0%	6.8%	9.0%	21.0%	42.8%	0.0%	3.0%	6.8%	9.8%	21.8%	42.8%
1924	0.0%	1.5%	3.0%	9.0%	25.0%	43.0%	0.0%	1.5%	3.0%	9.0%	24.0%	44.0%
1925	0.0%	1.1%	2.3%	7.5%	22.0%	25.0%	0.0%	1.1%	2.3%	7.5%	21.0%	25.0%
1926	0.0%	1.1%	2.3%	7.5%	22.0%	25.0%	0.0%	1.1%	2.3%	6.8%	21.0%	25.0%
1927	0.0%	1.1%	3.0%	7.5%	22.0%	25.0%	0.0%	1.1%	3.0%	7.5%	22.0%	25.0%
1928	0.0%	1.1%	3.0%	8.3%	24.0%	25.0%	0.0%	1.1%	3.0%	8.3%	23.0%	25.0%
1929	0.0%	1.1%	2.3%	6.8%	22.0%	24.0%	0.0%	1.1%	2.3%	6.8%	22.0%	24.0%
1930	0.0%	0.0%	1.1%	5.3%	17.0%	25.0%	0.0%	0.0%	2.3%	5.3%	17.0%	25.0%
1931	0.0%	0.0%	1.1%	3.0%	14.0%	25.0%	0.0%	0.0%	1.1%	3.0%	14.0%	25.0%
1932	0.0%	0.0%	4.0%	9.0%	19.0%	56.0%	0.0%	0.0%	4.0%	9.0%	19.0%	56.0%
1933	0.0%	0.0%	4.0%	9.0%	19.0%	56.0%	0.0%	0.0%	4.0%	9.0%	19.0%	56.0%
1934	0.0%	0.0%	4.0%	8.0%	21.0%	56.0%	0.0%	0.0%	4.0%	8.0%	23.0%	56.0%
1935	0.0%	0.0%	4.0%	9.0%	23.0%	56.0%	0.0%	0.0%	4.0%	9.0%	23.0%	56.0%
1936	0.0%	0.0%	4.0%	11.0%	28.0%	64.0%	0.0%	0.0%	4.0%	11.0%	28.0%	64.0%
1937	0.0%	0.0%	4.0%	10.0%	25.0%	64.0%	0.0%	0.0%	4.0%	11.0%	28.0%	64.0%

1938	0.0%	0.0%	4.0%	9.0%	23.0%	62.0%	0.0%	0.0%	4.0%	9.0%	23.0%	62.0%
1939	0.0%	0.0%	4.0%	9.0%	23.0%	62.0%	0.0%	0.0%	4.0%	10.0%	25.0%	62.0%
1940	0.0%	4.4%	4.4%	13.2%	40.7%	68.2%	0.0%	4.4%	4.4%	13.2%	40.7%	70.4%
1941	10.0%	10.0%	17.0%	33.0%	57.0%	70.0%	10.0%	10.0%	17.0%	33.0%	57.0%	70.0%
1942	19.6%	22.7%	30.9%	50.5%	71.1%	91.4%	19.6%	22.7%	30.9%	50.5%	72.5%	91.4%
1943	19.6%	22.7%	35.0%	53.6%	75.6%	91.4%	19.6%	22.7%	35.0%	53.6%	75.6%	91.4%
1944	25.0%	25.0%	37.0%	56.0%	75.0%	93.0%	23.0%	25.0%	37.0%	56.0%	75.0%	93.0%
1945	25.0%	29.0%	41.0%	59.0%	75.0%	92.0%	23.0%	25.0%	41.0%	56.0%	75.0%	93.0%
1946	20.9%	24.7%	40.9%	56.1%	71.3%	85.5%	20.9%	24.7%	40.9%	56.1%	71.3%	85.5%
1947	20.9%	24.7%	40.9%	56.1%	71.3%	85.5%	20.9%	24.7%	40.9%	56.1%	71.3%	85.5%
1948	19.4%	22.9%	37.8%	54.6%	68.6%	82.1%	19.4%	22.9%	41.4%	54.6%	68.6%	82.1%
1949	19.4%	22.9%	37.8%	51.9%	66.0%	82.1%	19.4%	22.9%	37.8%	51.9%	68.6%	82.1%
1950	20.0%	27.3%	42.8%	56.4%	73.7%	83.4%	20.0%	27.3%	42.8%	56.4%	73.7%	84.4%
1954	26.0%	30.0%	50.0%	62.0%	75.0%	90.0%	26.0%	30.0%	50.0%	62.0%	75.0%	90.0%
1956	22.0%	26.0%	34.0%	50.0%	62.0%	84.0%	22.0%	26.0%	34.0%	47.0%	62.0%	87.0%
1958	22.0%	26.0%	34.0%	50.0%	62.0%	84.0%	22.0%	26.0%	34.0%	47.0%	62.0%	84.0%
1960	22.8%	28.1%	39.1%	51.4%	62.9%	49.1%	22.7%	27.5%	38.3%	49.6%	64.5%	80.3%
1962	24.0%	29.2%	40.8%	52.8%	62.4%	55.2%	24.0%	28.5%	39.8%	50.8%	64.5%	79.7%
1964	22.8%	27.9%	38.8%	50.0%	58.0%	55.5%	22.7%	27.2%	38.0%	48.7%	59.7%	72.1%
1966	22.4%	27.4%	38.6%	48.5%	56.1%	53.2%	22.4%	26.7%	37.8%	47.1%	58.1%	67.4%
1968	25.6%	31.9%	45.0%	54.5%	60.0%	53.6%	25.4%	30.7%	43.7%	52.8%	64.0%	71.7%
1970	25.6%	31.2%	42.2%	50.5%	58.3%	55.8%	25.6%	30.5%	41.9%	50.3%	59.8%	67.1%
1972	25.7%	31.9%	42.8%	49.7%	56.8%	60.1%	25.6%	31.1%	42.5%	49.8%	59.4%	65.6%
1974	27.2%	33.7%	44.2%	50.8%	57.8%	60.5%	27.1%	33.1%	44.3%	51.2%	60.0%	65.2%
1975	28.7%	35.6%	45.9%	52.4%	59.3%	60.7%	28.6%	35.1%	46.3%	52.8%	61.1%	64.9%
1976	29.9%	36.9%	47.1%	52.9%	58.5%	54.8%	29.7%	36.3%	47.4%	53.6%	61.6%	65.7%

(*continued*)

Table 4.A3 Continued

	Fractiles defined including K gains						Fractiles defined excluding K gains					
	P90–95 (1)	P95–99 (2)	P99–99.5 (3)	P99.5–99.9 (4)	P99.9–99.99 (5)	P99.99–100 (6)	P90–95 (7)	P95–99 (8)	P99–99.5 (9)	P99.5–99.9 (10)	P99.9–99.99 (11)	P99.99–100 (12)
1977	30.3%	39.4%	50.7%	55.8%	62.6%	62.6%	30.1%	38.4%	50.8%	56.0%	63.5%	65.6%
1978	30.6%	38.9%	48.8%	54.3%	60.8%	62.0%	30.6%	38.2%	49.2%	54.9%	62.7%	65.9%
1979	33.3%	40.6%	48.7%	54.1%	57.8%	58.9%	33.1%	40.5%	49.7%	55.7%	62.8%	64.2%
1980	35.6%	42.6%	50.2%	55.1%	56.0%	44.4%	35.4%	42.3%	50.8%	56.5%	62.4%	63.0%
1981	37.3%	43.7%	49.9%	54.2%	53.2%	42.7%	37.4%	43.4%	51.0%	55.9%	60.8%	60.4%
1982	34.9%	40.9%	46.1%	46.4%	45.0%	42.0%	34.7%	40.6%	46.9%	48.3%	48.4%	47.6%
1983	32.5%	37.6%	42.1%	43.8%	43.1%	41.4%	32.4%	37.4%	42.9%	46.2%	47.8%	47.4%
1984	32.5%	37.6%	41.4%	43.6%	43.8%	41.5%	32.3%	37.4%	42.4%	45.7%	48.2%	47.9%
1985	33.2%	38.5%	43.0%	44.9%	44.6%	43.0%	33.0%	38.3%	43.6%	47.3%	48.9%	48.6%
1986	33.0%	37.8%	41.7%	42.2%	42.4%	41.7%	32.5%	37.7%	43.2%	46.4%	48.7%	48.5%
1987	31.1%	35.3%	37.8%	37.3%	37.1%	36.4%	30.6%	35.1%	38.7%	38.1%	38.0%	37.7%
1988	28.3%	30.9%	31.1%	27.8%	27.6%	27.4%	28.3%	30.2%	31.9%	28.2%	27.7%	27.6%
1989	28.3%	31.1%	31.2%	27.8%	27.6%	27.3%	28.3%	30.4%	31.7%	28.2%	27.6%	27.5%
1990	28.2%	31.0%	31.0%	27.6%	27.6%	27.3%	28.2%	30.4%	31.6%	27.9%	27.6%	27.4%
1991	27.9%	30.4%	33.6%	31.2%	30.9%	30.3%	27.8%	29.9%	33.7%	31.5%	31.1%	30.7%
1992	27.9%	29.9%	33.1%	30.8%	30.8%	30.3%	27.9%	29.4%	33.2%	31.0%	31.0%	30.6%
1993	28.2%	30.7%	37.9%	38.1%	38.5%	37.6%	28.2%	30.0%	38.0%	38.6%	39.6%	39.1%
1994	28.2%	30.9%	38.3%	38.6%	38.4%	37.3%	28.2%	30.2%	38.4%	39.1%	39.4%	38.9%
1995	28.2%	31.3%	37.8%	37.6%	37.9%	36.5%	28.2%	30.5%	37.9%	38.2%	39.2%	38.7%
1996	28.2%	31.3%	36.1%	35.9%	36.6%	34.7%	28.2%	30.4%	36.5%	36.4%	38.1%	37.9%
1997	28.2%	31.8%	37.0%	37.4%	37.3%	36.3%	28.2%	30.8%	37.3%	38.3%	38.9%	38.5%
1998	28.5%	32.6%	36.6%	37.1%	37.0%	35.8%	28.5%	31.7%	37.3%	38.4%	38.8%	38.7%
1999	28.9%	33.1%	36.4%	37.2%	37.1%	35.9%	28.7%	32.2%	37.2%	38.5%	38.8%	38.5%
2000	29.8%	33.5%	36.5%	37.3%	37.1%	35.7%	29.6%	32.7%	37.7%	38.8%	38.9%	38.6%
2001	29.0%	32.5%	36.5%	37.2%	37.2%	35.9%	28.9%	31.8%	37.1%	38.1%	38.5%	38.2%

Note: Marginal tax rates (MTR) are federal marginal income tax rates on net earned income for the primary earner.

Source: Authors' computation from own tax simulator for years prior to 1960 and from NBER Taxsim9 simulator for years after 1960.

MTR are computed for a couple filing jointly with two children and earning the average gross income in the income group, as interpolated from SOI tabulations.

All adjustments, deductions, and earned income credits are taken into account and are computed as average adjustments/deductions reported for the income group, as interpolated from SOI tabulations.

References

Ackerman, D. and G. Auten (2008), *Incentive and Distributional Consequences of Tax Expenditures.* (National Bureau of Economic Research) Cambridge, MA.

Allingham, M. G. and A. Sandmo (1972), "Income Tax Evasion: A Theoretical Analysis," *Journal of Public Economics, 1* (3–4), 323–338.

Andreoni, J. (2006), *Philanthropy*, Vol. 1 of *Handbook on the Economics of Giving, Reciprocity and Altruism* (Anderson: Elsevier).

Andreoni, J., B. Erard, and J. Feinstein (1998), "Tax Compliance," *Journal of Economic Literature, 36* (2), 818–860.

Atkinson, A. B. (1983), "The Income Tax Treatment of Charitable Contributions," in *Social Justice* and Public Policy (Cambridge MA: MIT Press).

Auten, G. E., H. Sieg, and C. T. Clotfelter (2002), "Charitable Giving, Income and Taxes: An Analysis of Panel Data," *American Economic Review, 92* (1), 371–382.

Bakija, J. (2000), "Distinguishing Transitory and Permanent Price Elasticities of Charitable Giving with Pre-announced Changes in Tax Law," *Working Paper* retrieved from http://web.williams.edu/Economics/wp/bakijacharity.pdf.

Bakija, J. and B. Heim (2011), "How Does Charitable Giving Respond to Incentives and Income? New Estimates from Panel Data," *National Tax Journal, 64* (2).

Barett, K. S., A. M. McGuirk, and R. Steinberg (1997), "Further Evidence of the Dynamic Impact of Taxes on Charitable Giving," *National Tax Journal, 50* (2), 321–334.

Bernheim, B. D. (2008), "Behavioral Welfare Economics," *NBER working paper series n.14622* (Cambridge, MA: NBER).

Bertrand, M., E. Duflo, and S. Mullainathan (2004), "How Much Should We Trust Differences-in-Differences Estimates?," *Quarterly Journal of Economics, 119* (1), 249–275.

Blumenthal, M., C. Christian, and J. Slemrod (1998), "The Determinants of Income Tax Compliance: Evidence from a Controlled Experiment in Minnesota," *NBER Working Papers n.6575*, (Cambridge, MA: NBER).

Blundell, R. and S. Bond (1998), "Initial Conditions and Moment Restrictions in Dynamic Panel Data Models," *Journal of Econometrics, 87*, 115–143.

Bradley, R., S. Holden, and R. McLelland (2005), "A Robust Estimation of the Effects of Taxation on Charitable Contributions," *Contemporary Economic Policy, 23*, 545–554.

Center on Philanthropy, ed. (2009), *The 2008 Study of High Net Worth Philanthropy: Issues Driving Charitable Activities among Affluent Households.*

Chetty, R. (2009a), "Is the Taxable Income Elasticity Sufficient to Calculate Deadweight Loss? The Implications of Evasion and Avoidance," *American Economic Journal: Economic Policy, 1*, 31–52.

Chetty, R. (2009b), "Sufficient Statistics for Welfare Analysis: A Bridge Between Structural and Reduced-Form Methods," *Annual Review of Economics*, (1), 451–488.

Clotfelter, C. T. (1980), "Tax Incentives and Charitable Giving: Evidence from a Panel of Taxpayers," *Journal of Public Economics, 13* (3), 319–340.

Clotfelter, C. T. (1983), "Tax Evasion and Tax Rates: An Analysis of Individual Returns," *The Review of Economics and Statistics, 65* (3), 363–373.

DellaVigna, S., J. List, and U. Malmendier (2009), "Testing for Altruism and Social Pressure in Charitable Giving." Mimeo UC Berkeley.

Diamond, P. (2006), "Optimal Tax Treatment of Private Contributions for Public Goods with and without Warm Glow Preferences," *Journal of Public Economics, 90* (4–5), 897–919.

Fack, G. and C. Landais (2010), "Are Fiscal Incentives for Charitable Contributions Efficient? Evidence from France," *American Economic Journal: Economic Policy, 2* (2): 117–141.

Fack, G. and C. Landais (2016), "The Effect of Tax Enforcement on Tax Elasticities: Evidence from Charitable Contributions in France," *Journal of Public Economics, 133*, 23–40.

Feinstein, J. S. (1991), "An Econometric Analysis of Income Tax Evasion and its Detection," *Rand Journal of Economics, 22* (1), 14–35.

Feldman, N. E. and J. Slemrod (2007), "Estimating Tax Noncompliance with Evidence from Unaudited Tax Returns," *Economic Journal, 117* (518), 327–352.

Feldstein, M. and A. Taylor (1976), "The Income Tax and Charitable Contributions," *Econometrica, 44* (6), 1201–1222.

Feldstein, M. and C. T. Clotfelter (1976), "Tax Incentives and Charitable Contributions in the United States : A Microeconometric Analysis," *Journal of Public Economics, 5* (1–2), 1–26.

Fisman, R. and S.-J. Wei (2004), "Tax Rates and Tax Evasion: Evidence from "Missing Imports" in China," *Journal of Political Economy, 112* (2), 471–500.

Gorodnichenko, Y., J. Martinez-Vazquez, and K. Sabirianova Peter (2009), "Myth and Reality of Flat Tax Reform: Micro Estimates of Tax Evasion Response and Welfare Effects in Russia," *Journal of Political Economy, 117* (3), 504–554.

Gruber, J. and D. M. Hungerman (2007), "Faith-based Charity and Crowd-out during the Great Depression," *Journal of Public Economics, 91* (5–6), 1043–1069.

Hsieh, C.-T. and E. Moretti (2006), "Did Iraq Cheat the United Nations? Underpricing, Bribes, and the Oil for Food Program," *Quarterly Journal of Economics, 121* (4), 1211–1248.

Hungerman, D. M. (2005), "Are Church and State Substitutes? Evidence from the 1996 Welfare Reform," *Journal of Public Economics, 89* (11–12), 2245–2267.

IRS, *Statistics of Income Bulletin*, July 2009, retrieved from http://www.irs.gov/pub/irs-soi/07in54cm.xls.

Kingma, B. (1989), "An Accurate Measurement of the Crowd-Out Effect, Income Effect, and Price Effect for Charitable Contributions," *Journal of Political Economy, 97* (5).

Klepper, S. and D. Nagin (1989), "The Anatomy of Tax Evasion," *Journal of Law, Economics and Organization, 5* (1), 1–24.

Kleven, H. J., C. T. Kreiner, and E. Saez (2009), "Why Can Modern Governments Tax So Much? An Agency Model of Firms as Fiscal Intermediaries," *NBER working paper series n.15218*. Cambridge, MA: NBER.

Kleven, H., M. Knudsen, K. Kreiner, S. Pederson, and E. Saez (2011), "Unwilling or Unable to Cheat? Evidence from a Randomized Tax Audit Experiment in Denmark," *Econometrica, 79* (3), 651–692.

LaLumia, S. and J. M. Sallee (2001), "The Value of Honesty: Empirical Estimates from the Case of the Missing Children," *NBER working paper series n.17247*, July Cambridge, MA: NBER.

Marion J. and E. Muehelegger (2008), 'Measuring illegal activity and the effects of regulatory innovation: tax evasion and the dyeing of untaxed diesel,' *Journal of Public Economics, 116* (4), 633–666.

Moulton, B. R. (1990), "An Illustration of a Pitfall in Estimating the Effects of Aggregate Variables on Micro Unit," *Review of Economics and Statistics, 72* (2), 334–338.

North, D., J. Wallis, and B. Weingast (2009), *Violence and Social Orders: A Conceptual Framework for Interpreting Recorded Human History* (Cambridge: Cambridge University Press).

Peterson, P. (1970), *Foundations, Private Giving and Public Policy: Report and Recommendations of the Commission on Foundations and Private Philanthropy* Chicago: University of Chicago Press.

Piketty, T. and E. Saez (2003), "Income Inequality in the United States, 1913–1998," *Quarterly Journal of Economics, 118* (1), 1–39.

Poterba, J. M (1987), "Tax Evasion and Capital Gains Taxation," *American Economic Review, 77* (2), 234–239.

Randolph, W. C. (1995), "Dynamic Income, Progressive Taxes, and the Timing of Charitable Contributions," *Journal of Political Economy, 103* (4), 700–738.

Roberts, R. D. (1987), "Financing Public Goods," *The Journal of Political Economy, 95* (2), 420–427.

Saez, E. (2004), "The Optimal Tax Treatment of Tax Expenditures," *Journal of Public Economics, 88*, 2657–2684.

Saez, E., J. B. Slemrod, and S. H. Giertz (2009), "The Elasticity of Taxable Income with Respect to Marginal Tax Rates: A Critical Review," *NBER Working Paper No. 15012*. Cambridge, MA: NBER.

Slemrod, J. B. (2006), "Taxation and Big Brother: Information, Personalization, and Privacy in 21st Century Tax Policy," *Fiscal Studies*, 27(1), 1–15.

Slemrod, J. B. (2007), "Cheating Ourselves: The Economics of Tax Evasion," *Journal of Economic Perspectives*, 25–48.

Slemrod, J. (1989), "Are Estimated Tax Elasticities Really Just Tax Evasion Elasticities? The Case of Charitable Contributions," *Review of Economics and Statistics, 71*(3), 517–522.

Turk, Alex, Maryamm Muzikir, Marsha Blumenthal, and Laura Kalambokidis (2007), "Charitable Contributions in a Voluntary Compliance Income Tax System: Itemized Deductions versus Matching Subsidies," in James Dalton and Martha Gangi, eds, *The IRS Research Bulletin: Proceedings of the 2007 IRS Research Conference*, US Internal Revenue Service Washington, DC, 51–74.

Warr, P. G. (1982), "Pareto Optimal Redistribution and Private Charity," *Journal of Public Economics, 19* (1), 131–138.

Wolfers, J. (2006), "Did Unilateral Divorce Laws Raise Divorce Rates? A Reconciliation and New Results," *American Economic Review, 96* (5), 1802–1820.

Yermack, D. (2008), "Deductio Ad Absurdum: CEOs Donating Their Own Stock to Their Own Family Foundations," Mimeo NYU Stern.

5

Charitable Donations and Tax Relief in the UK

Kimberley Scharf & Sarah Smith

5.1 Introduction

It is estimated that more than 50% of UK residents make charitable contributions each month;[1] private donations amount to three-quarters of a percentage point of gross domestic product (GDP), putting the UK second only to the US in the international giving league.[2]

The UK charitable sector has a long history; its current form dates back to the sixteenth century when, following the English Reformation, charity, which had previously been almost exclusively the domain of the Church, became increasingly organized along secular lines. Growing concern about poverty—and the social unrest it might create—resulted in the Elizabethan Poor Laws that enabled private charitable activities to evolve into an independent charitable sector, enjoying privileges and exemptions that were previously only afforded to the Church and to universities. Most sixteenth century private charities were hospitals (almshouses). These were individually funded by bequests or endowments and were intended solely to provide aid for the aged and impotent, not the sick. There were also numerous charities established to assist the young, mainly schools set up for the education of the young and endowed through bequests or gifts (and sometimes through the corporate action of towns). Later, under the influence of the Puritan movement, there was an increase in religious-oriented charities—bequests were made to fund religious

[1] UK Charities Aid Foundation, "World Giving Index 2010" in September 2010.

[2] UK Charities Aid Foundation, "International comparisons of charitable giving," November 2006.

Table 5.1 UK Charitable Sector, by Size of Organization

	Number of organizations	% organizations	% sector income	% income from individuals
Micro (<£10,000)	87,683	53.5%	0.6%	65%
Small (£10k–£100k)	51,090	31.2%	4.9%	50%
Medium (£100k–£1m)	20,432	12.5%	17.2%	38%
Large (£1m–£10m)	4,084	2.5%	30.9%	38%
(£10m+)	474	0.3%	46.4%	39%

Source: NCVO 2012. Note that the number of charities counted by the NCVO differs from the Charities Commission because they include charities in Scotland and Northern Ireland. They also exclude certain types of organizations, such as universities, housing associations, private schools.

lectures and the distribution of Bibles—but the majority of charities remained largely secular. Today the UK charitable sector consists of 160,000+ charities with a combined income in 2009/10 of £36.7 billion (2.5% of GDP) see table 5.1.[3] Of this income, £14.3 billion comes from individuals (£6.0 bn from unprompted donations, £4.3 bn from fees for services, £2.2 bn from donations in response to fundraising activities and £1.8 bn from legacies); £13.9 billion from statutory sources (£10.9 billion in contracts and fees and £3.0 in grants) and the remainder from investments and from trading. The activities of the sector remain distinctive, compared with the US—perhaps reflecting its sixteenth-century origins. Social services account for nearly one-quarter of total sector spending, followed by health (11.0%) and culture and recreation (10.5%). Religious organizations play a relatively small role in the UK charitable sector compared with the US (4.1% of all spending).

When income tax was introduced in 1799, charitable organizations were specifically exempted from paying the tax on the grounds that the activities of generated a "public benefit"—that is, relieved pressure from the public purse. Initially, there was no direct tax relief for private donations, but tax liability on money transferred through deed of covenant—a promise to make regular payments to a trust or individual over some period of time—could be transferred to the holder of the deed and, since charities were tax exempt, this was one way for individuals to avoid paying income tax on (regular) donations.

[3] This is part of a wider third sector, or civil society which is made up of an estimated 900,000 organizations including co-operatives, faith groups, clubs and societies, universities, housing associations, NHS charities, sports groups, and trades unions.

Gift Aid, which allows individuals to get tax relief on one-off donations to charity, was introduced in 1990. Its most distinctive feature is the presence of a match-style element, as well as the more familiar tax rebate element. Charities can claim basic rate income tax relief (at 20%) on donations, equivalent to a 25% match on gifts out of net-of-tax income. Higher-rate taxpayers can additionally reclaim a rebate on the difference between this and their marginal rate. In principle, both match and rebate affect the "price" of giving and, in a standard model, would be expected to affect giving in the same way. However, recent experimental evidence has suggested that this is not the case. Specifically, lab and field experiments summarized in Eckel and Grossman (2003, 2008), Davis, Millner, and Reiley (2005) and Blumenthal, Kalambokidis, and Turk (2012) have shown that offering donors a match has a bigger effect than an equivalent-value rebate on the total contributions (including the subsidy) received by the charity. These studies also find that total contributions are more responsive to variation in the match rate than to variation in the rebate rate. The UK provides an excellent setting to explore this potential asymmetry in relation to tax incentives. The focus of this chapter is a survey-based study of UK taxpayers that explores responses to (changes in) the match and rebate elements in Gift Aid. Section 5.2 describes tax reliefs on donations in the UK and Section 5.3 sets out a simple framework for understanding the effects of match and rebate incentives on giving. Section 5.4 describes the survey and the sample and Sections 5.5 and 5.6 presents the main results. Section 5.7 concludes.

5.2 Tax Relief on Giving

Table 5.2 summarizes the main forms of tax relief that individual donors can get on charitable donations in the UK.

Table 5.2 Tax Relief on Charitable Donations in the UK, 2010–2011

	Gross donations	Cost of tax relief
Gift Aid	£4,914 million	£1,435 million
Payroll Giving	£114 million	£30 million
Tax relief on shares or property	£266 million	£60 million
Legacies	£1,932 million	£460 million

Notes to table: The cost of Gift Aid tax relief comprises Gift Aid repayments to charities, including transitional relief payments, and the estimated cost of higher-rate relief.

Source: HM Revenue and Customs

5.2.1 *Gift Aid*

Gift Aid provides the main scheme through which individual taxpayers get tax relief on their donations to charity. The scheme was introduced in 1990, but with a minimum donation amount of £600, which was abolished in 2000. Gift Aid differs in operation to the US system of deductions and consists of the following two elements: (i) The charity can claim tax relief on donations made out of net-of-tax income at the basic rate of tax, currently 20%, which means that for every £1 donated to charity, the charity can reclaim 25 pence. This effectively works as a match-style incentive and is often marketed in this way by charities. (ii) In addition, higher-rate taxpayers can reclaim a rebate equal to the difference between the higher rate of tax (either 40% or 45%) and the basic rate of tax at 20% on the "gross" equivalent donation, i.e. the amount before basic rate tax was deducted. This means that for every £1 donated out of net income, a higher-rate taxpayer paying 40% can get an additional rebate of 25 pence. In accounting terms, this dual system is fully equivalent to a rebate system; the main reason why this was adopted had to do with administrative simplicity: basic-rate UK taxpayers are taxed on their income at source (through the "pay as you earn" system) without filing an income tax return.

Practically, charities claim back the basic rate relief on Gift Aid donations from HM Revenue and Customs by submitting a form with information on donor names and donation amounts. This can be done at any time up to four years after the donation has been made. Repayment to charities is usually made within four to five weeks. The claim must be backed by individual Gift Aid declarations in which donors declare that they want the charity to claim back the tax relief and they have paid sufficient tax. In each case, this must have the donors' name and address. In principle, the declaration can be made to the charity in writing or verbally. But, formally, charities are required to keep an audit trail that links the Gift Aid claim to individual declarations and must be able to demonstrate that the repayment claim is accurate. HMRC selects a limited number of charities for audit. In order for higher-rate taxpayers to receive the additional higher-rate rebate, they need to make a claim through a self-assessment tax return (completed by approximately a third of all UK taxpayers) or ask for a change in their tax code via a simpler tax review form.

In principle, charities and donors can overclaim. Only a limited number of charities are audited and the penalty for overclaiming is to pay back the amount over-claimed (plus interest). Also, to claim the rebate, higher-rate donors must keep records of their donations but are

Table 5.3 Estimated Proportion of Donations Attracting Tax Relief through Gift Aid

	Gross donations through Gift Aid	Estimated total individual donations	Proportion given through Gift Aid
2004–5	£2,842 million	£7,800 million	0.364
2005–6	£3,410 million	£9,400 million	0.363
2006–7	£3,771 million	£9,300 million	0.405
2007–8	£4,081 million	£10,600 million	0.385
2008–9	£4,299 million	£9,800 million	0.439
2009–10	£4,576 million	£10,600 million	0.432
2010–11	£4,914 million	£11,000 million	0.447

Notes to table: Estimates of total donations from NCVO

not required to provide HMRC with supporting evidence with every claim. However, the evidence suggests that, instead, there is substantial (net) under-claiming. The scale of this is illustrated in table 5.3 which compares total gross donations given through Gift Aid in recent years with estimates of the total amount given by individuals each year. This suggests that fewer than half of all donations attract tax relief, although this proportion has been increasing in recent years from 36% in 2004–05 to 45% in 2010–11. The degree of under-claiming may be linked to the administrative costs for charities, particularly the need for a Gift Aid declaration. The growth in online giving portals, which facilitate this declaration process, may help to explain the relative growth in Gift Aid donations. There are also administrative costs for higher-rate donors looking to reclaim a rebate since they need to fill in a self-assessment form or apply for a change in tax code.

It has been estimated that 35% of higher-rate donors actually reclaim. Information collected as part of our Gift Aid survey (described in more detail in section 5.3) suggests that lack of awareness is the main factor for why people do not reclaim. More than half of those who did not reclaim said that they did not know they could, while a further 32% of non-reclaimers said that they did not know how to claim back. The "hassle factor" also appears to be important. Nearly one-third of those who did not reclaim cited the time and effort it would take, while a further 19% said that it was too complicated. One-quarter said that they did not reclaim because they would only get a small amount of money back.

As expected, the probability of reclaiming is linked to the total amount given through Gift Aid. This relationship is shown in more detail in figure 5.1 which shows the proportion of higher-rate taxpayers who said that they reclaim, according to the size of Gift Aid donations.

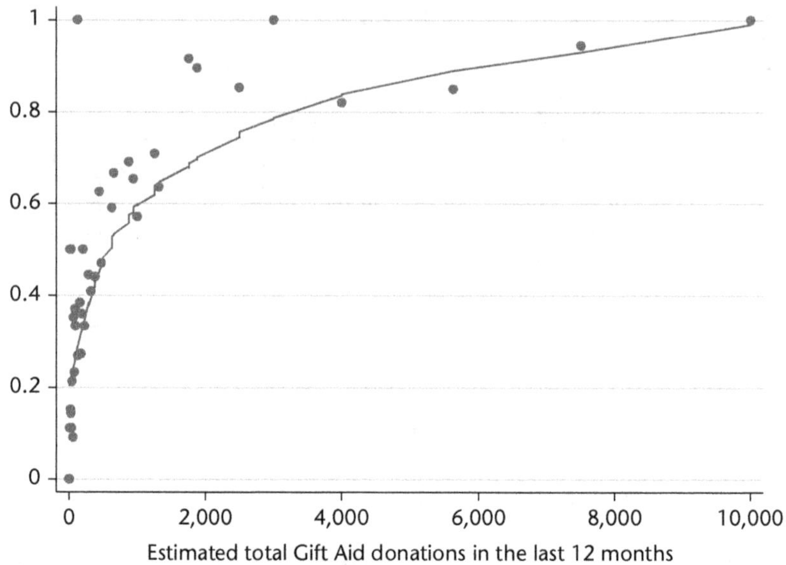

Figure 5.1 Proportion of Donors that Report Reclaiming the Rebate

This face that bigger donors are more likely to reclaim the rebate means that reclaimers account for an estimated 35% of higher-rate Gift Aid donors, but for nearly 80% of total Gift Aid donations made by higher-rate donors. People working part-time, the self-employed and those who are retired or not working are more likely to reclaim; this may be because they are more likely to complete a self-assessment form. Regular givers are more likely to reclaim.

5.2.2 *Payroll Giving*

Employees of firms that run payroll giving schemes can give to charity out of their gross earnings. The main benefit to a donor making charitable donations via a payroll giving scheme is the immediate tax relief at the time of making the donation. However, in spite of this administrative simplicity, take-up is low, even among employees of firms that run such schemes (where it is estimated that fewer than 6% participate).

5.2.3 *Gifts of Shares and Property*

Individual and corporate donors have been able to obtain income tax relief on gifts of shares and securities since 6 April 2000. This was extended in 2002 to cover a gift of land, and also applies to situations where a donor sells shares or property to a UK charity at less than market value. Relief is based on the market value of the gifted asset, which, additionally, is exempted from capitals gains taxation. This implies that transferring the asset to the charity involves a lower price of giving to a donor than selling the asset and transferring the receipts to the charity, in some instances significantly so. The tax relief in this case is always administered as a rebate (i.e. outside the Gift Aid scheme).

5.2.4 *Inheritance Tax*

Inheritance tax was introduced in 1984 replacing Capital Transfer Tax, which having been introduced in 1975 had imposed a tax charge on the gift of assets during the taxpayer's lifetime. The basic principle of inheritance taxation is that a tax charge arises on the reduction in the value of an individual's estate as a result of a transfer of an asset from the estate. There is a specific exemption from inheritance taxation where assets are given to charities, which applies equally to lifetime gifts and gifts on death. Additionally, an individual who receives a legacy can pass it on to a charity through a deed of variation within two years of the date of death of the deceased person; the gift is then treated as if it had been made by the deceased person (i.e. it is exempted from taxation).

5.3 Framework for Considering the Effects of Match and Rebate

To clarify our discussion of the effects of match and rebate incentives on contributions, consider the following simple model of charitable giving that has been used to underpin most empirical estimates of donor responses to changes in tax incentives for giving. We assume an economy of $i \in \{1, \ldots, N\}$ identical consumers, each of whom cares about their consumption of a private good, x_i, and their contribution towards the provision of a charitable good, g_i.

We assume that each consumer's preferences can be summarized by a well-behaved utility function, $U(x_i, g_i)$ and that each consumer has an exogenously given income, Y_i which can be used for consumption of the private good and for making checkbook donations, d_i, towards the charitable good, that is, each consumer's budget constraint is $Y_i = x_i + d_i$.[4]

[4] We also assume that the marginal rate of transformation in production between the private good and the charitable good is unity and we abstract from the public component

In the absence of any government subsidy, a checkbook donation from individual i translates into $g_i = d_i$ units of the charitable good, at a cost $c_i = d_i$ in terms of foregone spending on the private good. If there is a match, then the total contribution, received by the charity from each individual is equal to $g_i = (1 + m)d_i$, where m is the rate at which the checkbook donation, d_i, is matched by the government. In the UK, $m = 0.25$). If there is a rebate, the cost to each individual, ci, of making a nominal checkbook contribution, d_i, is equal to $c_i = (1 - r)d_i$ where r is equal to the rebate rate. In the UK, $r = 0.25$. The effect of this is to change each consumer's budget constraint to $Y_i = x_i + (1 - r)d_i$. To use the model to derive predictions on behavior, substitute $x_i = Y - (1 - r)d_i$ and $g_i = (1 + m)d_i$ into the utility function. Then, the consumer's optimization problem is to choose d_i so as to maximize $U(Y_i - (1 - r)d_i, (1 + m)d_i)$. The solution yields an optimal choice of checkbook donation, $d_i^* = D(p; Y)$ that is characterized by equality between the marginal rate of substitution between the charitable good and the private good and the price of giving, $p = (1 - r)/(1 + m)$.

Comparative static results show that $\frac{d\{(1+m)D^*(d;Y)\}}{dp} < 0$, i.e. $dg/dp < 0$. That is, the model predicts that an increase (decrease) in the price of giving will induce a decrease (increase) in total contributions. This result is independent of the instrument (match or rebate) that induces the change in price. If there is a switch from a match to an equivalent-value rebate, for example, then donors would be assumed to reduce their checkbook donation to preserve their total contribution.

However, US experimental studies conducted in the lab and the field have found that match and rebate subsidies do not affect total contributions in the same way. Eckel and Grossman (2003) carried out an experiment in the lab to test responses to equivalent-value match and rebates. Their experiment involved 181 undergraduate students who were each given twelve allocation problems—how to allocate an initial endowment between themselves and a charity of their choice when faced with varying amounts of the endowment and varying match and rebate rates. The first finding from these studies is that match subsidies result in a higher level of total contributions than equivalent-value rebates. Total contributions were 1.2–2 times greater with a match than a rebate. The second finding is that total contributions are more responsive to changes in the match than they are to changes in the rebate. The elasticity of total contributions with respect to changes in

of the charitable good by assuming that each consumer derives some private benefit from their contributions in the form of a warm-glow (Andreoni, 1990).

the price associated with changes in the match rate (which they call the match elasticity) is −1.14, while the elasticity with respect to changes in the price associated with changes in the rebate rate (which they call the rebate elasticity) is −0.36.[5]

Eckel and Grossman (2008) also ran an experiment in the field to test how donors responded to equivalent value match and rebates. On behalf of Minnesota Public Radio they mailed out 370,000+ donor solicitations, offering differing values of match rate and rebate on a random basis. The findings mirrored those from the lab. Based on approximately 7,000 responses, they found that the match rates resulted in a higher level of total contributions than equivalent-value rebates. The estimated elasticity of total contributions was −1.05 in the case of the match rate and −0.11 in the case of the rebate rate.

Experimental studies with similar findings on the asymmetry of the effect of match and rebate incentives have also been conducted by Davis, Millner, and Reiley (2005), Davis and Millner (2005), Davis (2006), Lukas, Grossman, and Eckel (2010) and Blumenthal, Kalambokidis, and Turk (2012).

There is also a related experimental literature which has explored how donors respond to match incentives funded by a significant lead donor (Karlan and List, 2007, Huck and Rasul, 2012). For example, Huck and Rasul (2012), test the effect of offering donors a 0.5 match and a 1.0 match, which are financed by a lead donor who allocates a fixed sum of money. They compare this with the effect of a lead donation of the same amount with no match and also to the effect of a simple request to give. They argue that this allows them to separately identify the effect of a lead donation from the "pure" price effect of varying the match, although this assumes that the effect of an unconditional lead donation is the same as using the lead donation to match and also that the effects of a lead donation and of price variation are additive.

The presence of a lead donation has a strong, positive effect on how much individuals donate (defined by checkbook donations and total contributions) compared to a simple request to give. A 0.5 match increases checkbook donations significantly compared to a simple request to give, but a 1.0 match does not. Under a 0.5 match, checkbook donations are not significantly different from an unconditional lead donation; under a 1.0 match, however, checkbook donations are

[5] They do not report that corresponding elasticities for checkbook donations, but these would be −0.14 in the case of the match and −0.36 in the case of the rebate.

significantly lower than an unconditional lead donation. Huck and Rasul (2012) interpret these findings as showing that lead donations significantly increase donations given, but that reducing the price of giving results in partial crowd-out. These findings contrast with those from the match/rebate studies, since the latter typically find elasticities with respect to total contributions that are greater than 1.0 in absolute value, implying crowd in of checkbook donations. The fact that Huck and Rasul (2012) combine the announcement of a lead donor with changes in the price may make their study hard to compare directly. A number of possible explanations have been given in the literature as to why match and rebate may have a different effect on total contributions (see Lukas, Grossman, and Eckel, 2010, for a discussion). One possibility is that consumers do not understand the implications of changes in the match and rebate rates for the price of giving. The fact, for example, that a match rate is higher in percentage terms than the equivalent value rebate may cause particular confusion (since $m = r/(1 - r)$). However, Davis and Millner (2005) show that the difference in responsiveness persists when donors are given information on the relationship between their checkbook donation, the total contribution to the charity and the net cost, suggesting that the difference cannot simply be attributed to confusion among donors.

Eckel and Grossman (2003, 2008) attribute the difference to preferences. Following Benabou and Tirole (2006) they argue that the match induces greater giving because it is associated with a cooperation frame, which makes donors feel more generous, while the rebate is associated with a reward frame.

In this chapter, we provide an alternative explanation that is more closely related to Davis (2006) who argue that the difference arises because, faced with a complex set of incentives, donors ignore both match and rebate and focus only on the checkbook donation. They refer to this as the "isolation" effect. In this case, the differential effect of match and rebate on total contributions arises purely as a mechanical consequence of ignoring (changes in) subsidies. Offering a match has a direct effect on g, while offering a rebate only affects the cost to the donor. Consistent with this, in our survey we find a high level of non-adjustment to changes in match and rebate subsidies. However, we show that there are important differences in the likelihood of adjusting depending on the level of giving and also on the type of incentive. We therefore argue that, rather than simply ignoring the match/rebate and focusing on the checkbook donation, donors do care about their total contribution but because of processing and adjustment costs may rationally choose to—or not to—process match and rebate in different situations, which is what is observed in practice. This kind of rational inattention has been discussed in relation to the salience of taxes that modify consumer prices (Chetty, Looney and Kroft, 2009) but the application to the effect of different forms of tax incentive that generate equivalent changes in the price (such as in our example of charitable giving)—and the implications for the design of effective tax subsidies—have not previously been explored.

Of course, there are a number of other stories about why people give that might explain a focus on checkbook donations. For example, donors might derive utility not from their total contribution but from the amount they give out of their net of tax income (their checkbook donation because it provides a more visible signal (see Glazer and Konrad, 1996; Harbaugh, 1998). However, in this case (as discussed in Turk et al., 2007), checkbook donations should be much more responsive to changes in the rebate (which affect the price of checkbook donations) than to changes in the match (which do not) and this is not observed in practice in most studies. Our survey also provides some additional evidence relevant to this issue—when asked about what they thought about when making their decision about how much to give, 69% of donors said that they thought about how much the charity claimed (on its own or together with how much they gave) compared with 13% who cared only about how much they gave and how much they could reclaim (the remaining 18% reported don't know). This suggests that an assumption that donors care about total contributions is appropriate for most givers.

5.4 Survey Evidence on Match and Rebate

We used a survey-based approach to explore how UK donors would respond to changes in the match and rebate elements of Gift Aid. Invitations to take part in an online survey were e-mailed to 40,000 UK-based donors, split equally between those who had donated online through Justgiving (an online giving portal) during the previous six months and those with a Charities Aid Foundation (CAF) charity account. 3,445 respondents were presented with a number of hypothetical scenarios involving changes to Gift Aid and asked to say how they would respond. The aim of the research was to explore a set of possible reforms to the existing system of Gift Aid that reduced the rebate element and increased the match element. The hypothetical scenarios were designed to reflect this and only higher-rate taxpayers faced options that changed both match and rebate elements (Gift Aid does not have a rebate element for basic-rate taxpayers). Our analysis therefore focuses on responses from just over 1,400 higher-rate donors.[6]

Before describing the research design in more detail, we address two potential concerns with our approach—first, that we do not sample from the general population of (Gift Aid) donors and second, that we use a stated choice approach.

Our data are drawn from a convenience sample comprising two groups. The first group is donors who have given through Justgiving, an online fundraising portal used primarily by individual fundraisers to collect sponsorship donations. The total population of Justgiving donors is around 20 million. The mean reported giving in the last 12 months among the sample respondents in this group who were higher-rate taxpayers is £2,377. The second group is people with a CAF charity account, an account that can be used to make donations and that facilitates tax-efficient giving. The total population of CAF account holders is around 60,000. The sample respondents from this group who were higher-rate taxpayers had mean reported giving of £4,846 in the last 12 months.

There is no reliable population information on Gift Aid donors that could act as a true benchmark for our sample. Even tax authority data is not fully comprehensive since many Gift Aid donors—including higher-rate donors—do not reclaim a rebate and do not therefore declare their giving. The best information is the Individual Giving Survey (IGS), a population-based survey that collects information on giving. Among the sample of higher-rate tax Gift Aid users in the IGS, the mean level of giving over the last 12 months was £1,411, lower than the mean of £3,332 in our combined Justgiving/CAF sample.

One issue is that we almost certainly over-sampled higher-rate taxpayers who reclaim the rebate—56% of our sample compared with an estimated 35% in the population. Re-weighting reduces the mean level of giving in our sample to £2,442 which is closer to the IGS figure, but still higher.

However, the IGS fails to capture major donors and is almost certainly likely to under-represent the level of giving—the largest donation was £46,000 in the last year in the IGS, compared with more than 100 donors who reported giving in excess of £100,000 in our sample. When we exclude donations of £50,000 or more and re-weight for our over-

[6] Note that no actual money was at stake. While individuals have been found to be differentially responsive to experiments depending on the amount of money at stake, it is unclear to what extent this absence of money at stake in our setting affects the relative responsiveness of individuals to a match vs a rebate.

sampling of reclaimers, the mean level of giving in the Justgiving/CAF sample falls to £1,796, which is much closer to the IGS figure.

We are therefore confident that our sample is broadly representative of the relevant population of higher-rate Gift Aid donors, once we take into account the higher proportion of reclaimers and the presence of major donors in our sample. In our analysis, we look separately at reclaimers and non-reclaimers and we also look at responses to match and rebate among different quartiles of the donor population.

The second potential issue is our use of a stated choice approach, which is not common in policy evaluation (although Krueger and Kuziemko (2011) provide an example). Ideally, we would like to look at responses to real tax changes, through either a field or natural experiment. However, field experiments involving tax rates are not feasible; nor is there any data on actual reforms that have taken place that is available and detailed enough. In the absence of evidence on actual tax policy changes, our survey approach complements existing experimental results but offers some potential advantages over alternatives in the lab or single-charity field studies. As discussed, we were able to survey the relevant population, resulting in a reasonably representative sample of higher-rate Gift Aid donors; and we were able to test donor responses to the relevant instrument, that is, tax incentives. Our survey approach allowed us to collect information on a large sample of donors and test for differential responses across donor groups, allowing us to explore alternative explanations for why total contributions respond differently to match and rebate subsidies.

We incorporated a number of elements into our survey design to make the findings more credible. We made the scenarios more realistic by asking respondents to consider how the alternative tax treatments would affect a specific donation that they had previously in the survey said that they were likely to make in the next six months rather than asking generally how they would respond to a change in tax incentives. We also use only within-person variation to identify the effects of match and rebate. In a recent paper, Johansson-Stenman and Svedsäter (2008) show in relation to contingent valuation studies that this is more robust than cross-person identification, arguing that people strive for consistency in their statements.[7] As a measure of the reliability of our

[7] Our study differs from a classic WTP study where, according to Harrison and Rutström (2008) "as a matter of logic, if you do not have to pay for the good but a higher verbal willingness to pay (WTP) response increases the chance of its provision, then verbalize away to increase your expected utility!" In our case, it is not clear *ex ante* whether donors would overstate since they are directly informed in the survey about tax changes and incur no real adjustment costs, or understate since a no adjustment response is the easiest answer to give.

survey responses, we can show that there is close agreement between how much CAF respondents in our sample reported they gave through Gift Aid during the last year (mean = £2,435) and how much was actually given by (the population of) CAF donors through CAF charity accounts during that year (mean = £2,436). We also show that the ordering of the options does not affect the responses, ruling out the so-called embedding effects (i.e the idea that the ordering of the scenarios may affect responses) discussed in Diamond and Hausman (1994).

The design of our scenarios was as follows. Respondents were first asked whether they were likely to make a Gift Aid donation in the next six months. Higher-rate taxpayers were then randomly allocated to five different treatment sets, each consisting of two hypothetical scenarios reflecting different combinations of match and rebate (summarized in the first column of table 5.4). In each case, respondents were asked to say how much they would give if faced with the alternative system of tax relief (see Appendix 5.A1 for further details on how the scenarios appeared in the survey).

The design and description of the scenarios in the survey reflect the way Gift Aid is portrayed to donors—that is, the charity receives X pence for every £1 given out of net-of-tax income and the individual can reclaim X pence for every £1 given out of net-of-tax income. For higher-rate taxpayers, two of the treatment sets (A, B) tested how people would respond to changes in either the match or the rebate (but not both).

In Set A, individuals were faced with the following two scenarios:

A1: A match of 30 pence and a rebate of 25 pence (price of giving = 0.577);

A2: A match of 25 pence and a rebate of 30 pence (price of giving = 0.560).

While in set B, individuals were faced with the following two scenarios:

B1: A match of 20 pence and a rebate of 25 pence (price of giving = 0.625);

B2: A match of 25 pence and a rebate of 20 pence (price of giving = 0.640).

Note that the changes in match and rebate were symmetric in terms of pence change for each £1 donated but not in terms of price changes. The price changes are larger for the changes in rebate. Eckel and Grossman (2003, 2008) defined match and rebate pairs that were equivalent in value but had different rates—for example, a 25% match and a 20%

Table 5.4 The Effect of Alternative Tax Treatments

Treatment		Price	N	Regression results: Dependent variable = total contribution (ln g_i)			Regression results: Dependent variable = checkbook donation (ln d_i)			Proportion adjusting checkbook donation (d_i)
				Coeff		SE	Coeff		SE	
Baseline	M = £0.25; R =£ 0.25	0.600								
A1	M = £0.30; R =£ 0.25	0.577	283	0.054	**	(0.005)	0.014	**	(0.005)	0.102
A2	M = £0.25; R = £0.30	0.560	283	0.033	**	(0.005)	0.033	**	(0.005)	0.244
B1	M = £0.20; R = £0.25	0.625	289	–0.040	**	(0.005)	0.001		(0.005)	0.069
B2	M = £0.25; R = £0.20	0.640	289	–0.006		(0.005)	–0.006		(0.005)	0.138
E1	M = £0.66; R = 0	0.600	267	0.276	**	(0.004)	–0.011	**	(0.004)	0.206
C1, E2	M = £0.50; R = 0	0.667	545	0.173	**	(0.003)	–0.009	**	(0.003)	0.196
D2	M = £0.37; R = 0	0.730	281	0.068	**	(0.004)	–0.024	**	(0.004)	0.228
C2, D1	M = £0.30; R = 0	0.769	559	0.009	**	(0.003)	–0.030	**	(0.003)	0.170

Note: The total contribution refers to the total amount of funding received by the charity (including the value of the match). The checkbook donation refers to the amount given out of net-of-tax income, without taking account of the match and before the donors has reclaimed any rebate. ** $p < 0.05$

rebate. However, experimental evidence shows that individuals respond differently to alternatives that produce exactly the same outcome but that are presented to them through what Kahneman and Tversky (1979) refer to as different "frames of reference" which may imply that donors respond more to what they perceive is a "larger" match. In our case, if the match and rebate elasticities are the same, there should be a larger percentage change in total contributions to the rebate change. If we find that total contributions respond less to the rebate change this is a strong indication that total contributions are less responsive to changes in the rebate than to changes in the match. The other treatment sets for higher-rate taxpayers (C, D, and E) were designed to explore responses to specific policy options that involved increasing the generosity of the match rate, while abolishing the rebate rate. Scenario E1 changed the form of the tax subsidy but not the price. The other scenarios involved increases in the price of giving compared with the current system. The same scenarios were included twice (C1 and E2 and C2 and D1) to test for embedding effects. Specifically, in Set C, individuals were faced with the following two scenarios:

C1: A match of 50 pence and no rebate (price of giving = 0.667);
C2: A match of 30 pence and no rebate (price of giving = 0.769).

In set D, individuals were faced with the following two scenarios:

D1: A match of 30 pence and no rebate (price of giving = 0.769);
D2: A match of 37 pence and no rebate (price of giving = 0.730).

While in set E, individuals were faced with the following two scenarios:

E1: A match of 66 pence and no rebate (price of giving = 0.600);
E2: A match of 50 pence and no rebate (price of giving = 0.667).

5.5 Results

To explore the effect of the different treatments on contributions, we estimate the following reduced form model:

$$\log g_{in} = \beta_0 + \sum_{s=1}^{S} \beta_s T_{si} + \nu_{in} \tag{5.1}$$

where g_{in} is the n-th contribution of individual i. For each donor, we observe up to three contributions—their initial total contribution, g_{i0}, and their contributions under the two different scenarios they face in their randomly allocated treatment set, that is, $n = 0, 1, 2$.

We choose to focus on the total contribution—the checkbook donation plus any match—for a number of reasons. The total contribution is relevant for the public policy debate; it is what previous analyses have typically focused on and, as discussed in Section 5.3, it is also what donors are assumed to care about. Although donors directly choose the level of their checkbook donation, they are assumed to adjust their checkbook donation to take account of the match or rebate to achieve the desired total contribution. However, we also report results for checkbook donations, *d*.

We include a set of binary indicators for each of the hypothetical scenarios ($T_{1i} = 1$ if $m = 0.30$ and $r = 0.25$ and $T_{1i} = 0$ otherwise; $T_{2i} = 1$ if $m = 0.25$ and $r = 0.30$ and $T_{2i} = 0$ otherwise; and so on). In total there were ten scenarios, but two of these simply involved varying the ordering of the scenarios in order to test for so-called embedding effects. Since the ordering made no significant difference to responses, our results focus on the eight distinct scenarios ($S = 8$). The error term is decomposed into a constant, individual-specific effect and a donation-specific random error term that could capture eg rounding or reporting error for each individual for each scenario they face, namely $\nu_{in} = \alpha_i + u_{in}$. The results from estimating equation 5.1 using a random effects model are reported in table 5.4.[8]

In line with earlier studies, we find that total contributions are more responsive to changes in the match than to changes in the rebate. Scenario A1 (M = 0.30; R = 0.25) is associated with a bigger increase in total contributions than scenario A2 (M = 0.25; R = 0.30), although the price reduction is smaller. Similarly, scenario B1 (M = 0.20; R = 0.25) is associated with a bigger fall in total contributions than scenario B2 (M = 0.25; R = 0.20), although the price increase is smaller. The coefficients associated with scenarios C1-E2 show that policy options that withdraw the rebate and increase the match result in an overall increase in total contributions, even where the price of giving has increased relative to the current system. The final column of table 5.4 summarizes the proportion of donors who, for each scenario, report that they would leave their checkbook donation (i.e. how much they give out of net-of-tax income) unchanged. Levels of non-adjustment are very high—the majority of donors for each scenario. As already discussed, and as we explore further in the next section, this non-adjustment is a key factor in understanding why total contributions respond more to changes in the match than to changes in the rebate.

[8] This is efficient and unbiased if the rebate and match terms are unrelated to individuals' characteristics. Since the rebate and match terms are randomly allocated to individuals this should be true by assumption. Very similar results were obtained from a fixed-effects model.

A potential concern is that this high level of non-adjustment may be an artifact of the hypothetical nature of the survey; there is no benefit to respondents if they respond truthfully and reporting an alternative donation amount may have a small effort/computational cost. However, as evidence against this, the proportion adjusting does vary across the scenarios—the proportion adjusting to changes in the rebate is typically greater than the proportion adjusting to changes in the match and more people adjust to a larger change in the match rate. In many cases, these differences in the level of non-adjustment across scenarios arise because the same individual reports that they will adjust in the case of one of the scenarios and not the other, consistent with respondents taking these scenarios seriously. We therefore have reason to believe this finding on non-adjustment is valid. The differences in levels of non-adjustment across scenarios also suggests that there is more going on than Davis (2006) isolation effect in which donors simply ignore (changes in) match and rebate rates altogether.

5.6 Heterogeneity of Responses across Donors

In order to facilitate direct comparisons with earlier studies and to allow convenient analysis for sub-groups of donors, we estimate separate price elasticities for price changes associated with changes in the match rate and changes in the rebate rate (referred to by Eckel and Grossman as match and rebate elasticities). We focus on scenarios A1–B2 which change either the match or the rebate. We estimate regressions of the following form:

$$\log g_{in} = \beta_0 + \beta_r \log(1 - r_s) + \beta_m \log(1 + m_s) + \nu_{in} \tag{5.2}$$

As before, we focus on total contributions. The terms β_r and β_m capture the elasticity of total contributions with respect to changes in the price through the rebate and match respectively. The basic results are reported in table 5.5, panel a. The magnitudes of the estimated elasticities, –1.12 in the case of the match and –0.22 in the case of the rebate, are very similar to those from Eckel and Grossman's experimental studies, –1.14–1.05 for the match and –0.36–0.11 for the rebate. Our results provide evidence that the asymmetry of responses holds with respect to match and rebate subsidies in the tax system. In addition, we can exploit additional information on the donors collected as part of the survey to explore potential explanations for why the responses are different.

Table 5.5 Elasticity Estimates

	Estimated match elasticity	Estimated rebate elasticity	P-value
All higher-rate taxpayers	–1.127 (*0.067*)	–0.212 (*0.041*)	0.0000
Whether or not individual reclaims higher-rate rebate			
Reclaimers	–1.277 (*0.096*)	–0.415 (*0.091*)	0.0000
Non-reclaimers	–0.946 (*0.091*)	0.032 (*0.054*)	0.0000
Level of understanding (higher-rate reclaimers)			
"Good"	–1.368 (*0.116*)	–0.440 (*0.070*)	0.0000
"Poor"	–1.095 (*0.170*)	–0.366 (*0.102*)	0.0000
Size of donations (higher-rate reclaimers)			
Quartile 1: £334	–1.177 (*0.220*)	–0.473 (*0.132*)	0.0002
Quartile 2: £1,056	–1.220 (*0.170*)	–0.277 (*0.119*)	0.0000
Quartile 3: £2,951	–1.154 (*0.180*)	–0.366 (*0.110*)	0.0000
Quartile 4: £20,193	–1.496 (*0.202*)	–0.559 (*0.123*)	0.0000
Whether or not donor adjusts checkbook donations (higher rate reclaimers)			
Adjusters	–1.929 (*0.297*)	–1.431 (*0.179*)	0.0581

Notes: standard errors in parentheses, p-value is for the test that the match and rebate elasticity are equal. Each line represents a separate regression.

5.6.1 *Reclaimers versus Non-reclaimers*

One possible explanation for why total contributions are more responsive to the match than to the rebate may be because of the additional processing cost for the donor associated with reclaiming the rebate. We explore this by comparing responses among reclaimers and non-reclaimers. We find that the presence of many non-reclaimers cannot account for the higher match elasticity. As shown in table 5.5, the estimated rebate elasticity among reclaimers is higher than among non-reclaimers, as would be expected (–0.415 compared with 0.032). However, among reclaimers, the estimated match elasticity is –1.277, significantly higher than the rebate elasticity.[9]

5.6.2 *Level of Understanding*

Here, we analyze the responses separately for donors according to their likely level of understanding of tax incentives. This is assessed on the basis of their response to a question about how much the match is worth to charities. Respondents are told that the charity can reclaim basic-rate tax and asked to say how much the charity gets for each

[9] We did not directly ask whether changes in the rebate affected the decision to reclaim; we therefore split the sample by whether people currently reclaim or not.

£1 donated out of net-of-tax income (choosing one out of a set of possible responses). If they respond correctly, we define them as having a good level of understanding. If they do not choose the correct answer, we define them as having a poor level of understanding. We find some difference between those with "good" and "poor" understanding—those with a good understanding are more responsive to changes in both match and rebate. Nevertheless, we find that the match elasticity is significantly higher than the rebate elasticity for both groups. This confirms the earlier findings from Davis, Millner, and Reiley (2005) that misunderstanding of the subsidies does not appear to be a plausible candidate explanation.

5.6.3 *Size of Contributions*

Table 5.5 also shows elasticity estimates by quartile of contributions. We find that total contributions from larger donors are more sensitive to changes in the rebate than total contributions from smaller donors but the significant difference in responsiveness of total contributions to match and rebate persists among all groups.

5.6.4 *Adjusters/Non-adjusters*

Non-adjustment of checkbook donations to changes in the match/rebate is potentially important for understanding why total contributions are more responsive to the match than to the rebate. This is because of the way that non-adjustment differentially impacts on total contributions in the two cases. If donors do not adjust their checkbook donation when the match changes, their total contributions automatically adjust (i.e. the elasticity of contributions is one in absolute value). If consumers do not adjust to a change in the rebate, on the other hand, there is no effect on their total contribution (i.e. the elasticity is equal to zero), rather the net cost to the donor adjusts. Non-adjustment can therefore generate higher contribution elasticities for the match than for the rebate.

Table 5.5 shows estimates of match and rebate elasticities separately for adjusters (i.e. donors who adjust to at least one of the two scenarios). For this group, total contributions are much more responsive to changes in the rebate compared to the rest of the sample. While the match elasticity is still higher than the rebate elasticity, the difference is no longer statistically significant. This suggests that non-adjustment is a big part of the explanation for why total contributions respond more to changes in the match than to changes in the rebate.

Davis (2006) provides an explanation that donors ignore match and rebate changes altogether and focus only on checkbook donations because the incentives are too complex. However, this does not explain why some donors do adjust. We propose a slightly different interpretation as follows (see Scharf and Smith (2011) for more detail). Suppose that donors do not simply ignore match and rebate changes but instead do care about their total contribution but (rationally) choose to respond to match and rebate changes and adjust their checkbook donations only when the benefits from doing so are greater than the costs. There may be some small effort costs involved in processing changes in tax relief and in adjusting checkbook donations. The cost of not adjusting is that donors' total contributions are further away from the optimal level. Chetty, Looney, and Kroft (2009) have shown that even small processing or adjustment costs can result in non-adjustment since such utility costs from failing to process tax changes are second order. However, donors would be more likely to adjust when the utility costs are higher.

We present two pieces of evidence in support of this story of donor "rational inattention." First, we show in figure 5.2 that the probability of adjusting is increasing in the size of contributions. This would be the case if, as seems likely, the utility costs of non-adjustment were relative

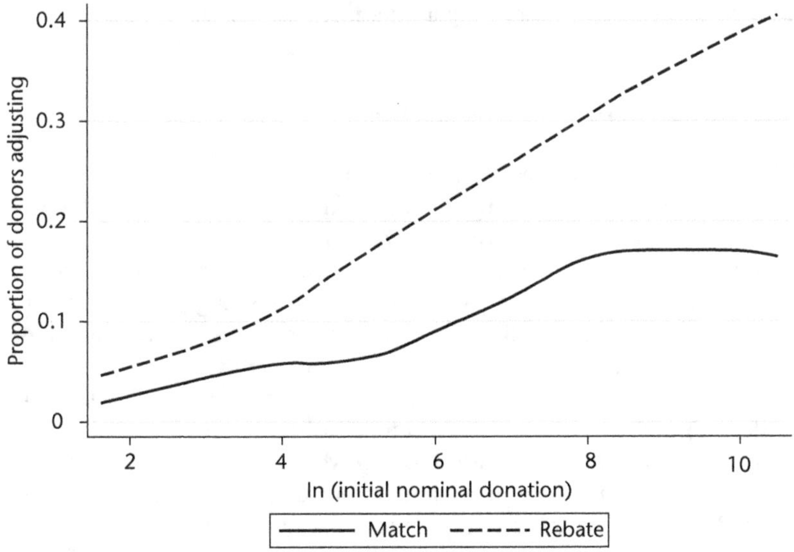

Figure 5.2 Proportion of Donors Adjusting Checkbook Donations

to the size of contribution while the processing costs were fixed in absolute terms. Second, the probability of adjusting is also consistently higher in the case of changes to the rebate than in the case of changes to the match. This would be the case if the costs of non-adjustment were greater for changes to the rebate than for changes to the match—which in turn would be the case if, absent any processing costs, total contributions were fairly price responsive. The intuition for this is that in the case of the match, total contributions automatically adjust in line with a change in the price while, in the case of the rebate, the donor has to adjust the checkbook donation for total contributions to change.

Of course, as discussed, there are other possible explanations in the literature on giving for why donors might not adjust their checkbook donation. One possibility is that donors care only about checkbook donations because they want to signal their wealth or generosity (Glazer and Konrad, 1996; Harbaugh, 1998). In this case, checkbook donations would respond more to a change in the rebate (which changes the price of such a signal) than to a change in the match (which does not). In practice, we cannot reject that the elasticity of checkbook donations with respect to the match is the same as the elasticity with respect to the rebate. Explanations which assume that donors care only about checkbook donations are less consistent with the observed patterns in the data than our rational inattention story in which donors care about the total contribution but do not always adjust their checkbook donation because of processing and adjustment costs.

5.7 Conclusions and Policy Implications

The survey evidence presented here complements the existing experimental studies in confirming the differential effect of match and rebate subsidies, in particular by showing that this difference holds when the incentives are offered through the tax system. This has clear policy implications. The asymmetry of responses strongly suggests that match-style tax incentives are likely to be more effective than rebate-style incentives if the objective is to increase total contributions.

However, replacing the current match and rebate elements of Gift Aid with a higher match rate could come at a higher cost for the government not only because a higher match would be more generous than the current system for non-reclaimers but also because reclaimers do not reduce their checkbook donations. A key question for policy-makers is whether it is possible to introduce a revenue-neutral policy change that will lead to an increase in the amount of money going to charities.

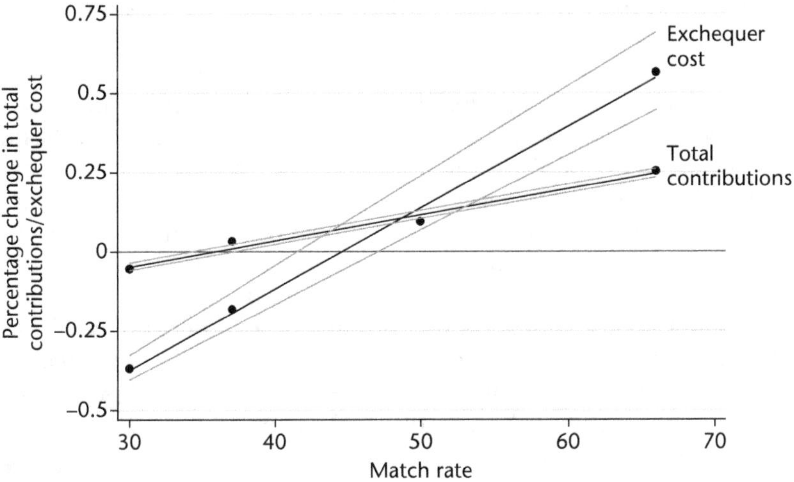

Figure 5.3 Estimated Change in Total Contributions and Cost of Tax Relief Associated with Match-Only Options

Notes: The central, bold line indicates the percentage changes in total contributions and the cost of tax relief compared to the current system based on an assumption that 35% of higher-rate taxpayers reclaim the rebate. The paler lines show the same, assuming that 25% and 45% reclaim.

To provide some further insight into this, figure 5.3 shows indicative estimates of the likely overall effect on total contributions and the estimated percentage change in the cost of tax relief for each of the four scenarios that involved withdrawing the rebate and increasing the value of the match for higher-rate donors—£0.30, £0.37, £0.50 and £0.66—together with smoothed, linear predictions through these point estimates. These take into account adjustments by reclaimers and non-reclaimers from the survey and the relative proportions of the two groups in the population of Gift Aid donors.

The results give an indication that it would be possible to increase gross donations, without increasing the cost of tax relief compared with the current system—by withdrawing the rebate and replacing it with a match in the range £0.42 to £0.47, depending on the proportion of higher-rate reclaimers. Alternatively, there is a possible policy change that maintains the current level of gross donations but with a cost saving (a match of £0.35). The form of tax incentive—and the differential responses to match and rebate—therefore should be taken into account in the design of public policy.

"Rational inattention"—the idea that small processing and adjustment costs may stop donors from adjusting their checkbook donations—also has a number of other implications for policy. The evidence shows that contributions from larger donors are more sensitive to changes in tax incentives than contributions from smaller donors hence targeting incentives on this group is likely to be more cost-effective. Bigger changes in tax rates are also likely to have relatively more impact. Relevant to this, the UK government announced a £50,000 cap on tax relief for donations in the March 2012 UK Budget. This would withdraw tax relief for donations in excess of £200,000 a year, which would be precisely the group that would be likely to be more responsive to tax incentives (in our survey the rebate elasticity among donors giving more than £100,000 a year was more than one in absolute value). Two months later, after a fierce debate, the proposal was dropped.

Acknowledgments

We would like to thank Charities Aid Foundation and Justgiving who allowed us to survey their donors. We have received helpful comments and suggestions from Abigail Payne and Camille Landais and participants at the CEPR conference on altruism. All remaining errors are our own. Note that a more detailed and extensive version of the analysis conducted in sections 5.3 to 5.5 can be found in "The Price Elasticity of Charitable Giving: Does the Form of Tax Relief Matter?," *International Tax and Public Finance* 22 (2), April 2015: 330–352.

Appendix 5.A1: Presentation of the Scenarios

Initial donation

How likely are you to make any Gift Aid donations to a charity within the next six months? This could be a one-off donation or a regular donation set up as a standing order or direct debit.

- Certain
- Very likely
- Fairly likely
- Not very likely
- Not at all likely
- Don't know

IF "Certain" or "Very likely" or "Fairly likely"
And how much do you think that you are likely to give (to the nearest pound)? If the donation you are thinking about is a regular direct debit or standing order, please give the total of that donation for a six month period.

Introduction to scenarios

The Gift Aid scheme allows charities to reclaim the basic rate income tax on your donation and allows higher rate taxpayers to claim back higher rate tax relief. You are now going to be presented with two hypothetical changes to the Gift Aid scheme – either to the amount that the charity can reclaim and/or to the amount that higher rate taxpayers can claim back. In each case you will be asked to consider whether the amount of money that you are likely to give to charity would be affected by the proposed changes.

Example

Through the Gift Aid scheme, the charity you are donating to reclaims the basic rate income tax on your donation. This is worth 25 pence for every £1 you donate.

Suppose instead that the charity received 30 pence for every £1 you donate. (Assume that the amount of higher rate relief that you can claim back is unchanged.)

Thinking about your donation of [£X] would this change affect the amount you are likely to give? SINGLE CODE ONLY

- Yes - I would give more than [£X]
- Yes - I would give less than [£X]
- No - I would give the same amount
- Don't know

IF yes, how much would you be likely to give (to the nearest pound)?

- (write in)
- Don't know

IF 'don't know', which of these comes closest to what you think you might increase/reduce your donation by?

- By 10% or less?
- By more than 10%?
- Don't know

If more than 10%, would you increase/reduce your donation by 25% or more?

- Yes
- No
- Don't know

If yes, would you increase/reduce your donation by 50% or more?

- Yes
- No
- Don't know

References

Andreoni, J. (1990), "Impure Altruism and Donations to Public Goods: A Theory of Warm-Glow Giving," *Economic Journal 100*: 464–477.

Bénabou, R. and J. Tirole (2006), "Belief in a Just World and Redistributive Politics," The Quarterly Journal of Economics, 121 (2), 699–746.

Blumenthal, M., L. Kalambokidis, and A. Turk (2012), "Subsidizing Charitable Contributions with a Match Instead of a Deduction: What Happens to Donations and Compliance?" *National Tax Journal 65*: 91–116.

Chetty, R., A. Looney, and K. Kroft (2009), "Salience and Taxation: Theory and Evidence," *American Economic Review 99*: 1145–1177.

Diamond, P. and J. Hausman (1994), "Contingent Valuation: Is Some Number Better Than No Number?" *Journal of Economic Perspectives 8*: 45–64.

Davis, D. and E. Millner (2005), "Rebates and Matches and Consumer Behavior," *Southern Economic Journal* 72: 410–421.

Davis, D., E. Millner, and R. Reiley (2005), "Subsidy Schemes and Charitable Contributions: A Closer Look," *Experimental Economics 8*: 85–106.

Davis, D. (2006), "Rebate Subsidies, Matching Subsidies and Isolation Effects," *Judgment and Decision-Making 1*: 13–22.

Eckel, C. and P. Grossman (2003), "Rebate Versus Matching? Does how we Subsidize Charitable Contributions Matter?" *Journal of Public Economics 87*: 681–701.

Eckel, C. and P. Grossman (2008), "Subsidizing Charitable Contributions: A Natural Field Experiment Comparing Matching and Rebate Subsidies,"' *Experimental Economics 11*: 234–252.

Glazer, Amihai and Kai Konrad (1996), "A Signaling Explanation for Charity," *American Economic Review 86*: 1019–1028.

Harbaugh, William (1998), "The Prestige Motive for Making Charitable Transfers," *American Economic Review, Papers and Proceedings 88*: 277–82.

Harrison, G. and E. Rutsrom (2006), "Hypothetical Bias Over Uncertain Outcomes," in J. List, (ed.), *Using Experimental Methods in Environmental and Resource Economics* (Northampton, MA: Edwad Elgar).

Huck, S. and I. Rasul (2012), "Matched Fundraising: Evidence from a Natural Field Experiment," *Journal of Public Economics 95*: 351–362.

Johansson-Stenman, O. and H. Svedsäter (2008), "Measuring Hypothetical Bias in Choice Experiments: The Importance of Cognitive Consistency," *The B.E. Journal of Economic Analysis & Policy 8*, Article 41.

Kahneman, D. and A. Tversky (1979), "Prospect Theory: An Analysis of Decision under Risk," Econometrica, 47 (2), 263–91.

Karlan, D. and J. List (2007), "Does Price Matter in Charitable Giving? Evidence from a Large-scale Natural Field Experiment," *American Economic Review 97*: 1774–1793.

Krueger, A. and I. Kuziemko (2011), "The Demand for Health Insurance Among Uninsured Americans: Results of a Survey Experiment and Implications for Policy," *NBER working paper* 16978. Cambridge, MA: NBER.

Lukas, I., P. Grossman, and C. Eckel (2010), "Preference or Confusion: Understanding the Differential Impact of Rebate and Matching Subsidies," Working Paper. Indiana University, Indianapolis, IN.

Scharf, K. and S. Smith (2011), "Rational Inattention to Subsidies for Charitable Contributions," CEPR discussion paper 7760.

Turk, Alex, Maryamm Muzikir, Marsha Blumenthal and Laura Kalambokidis (2007), "Charitable Contributions in a Voluntary Compliance Income Tax System: Itemized Deductions versus Matching Subsidies," in James Dalton and Martha Gangi, eds, *The IRS Research Bulletin: Proceedings of the 2007 IRS Research Conference*, US Internal Revenue Service Washington, DC, 51–74.

Name Index

Note: includes all referenced authors

Subject Index

Tables and figures are indicated by an italic *t* and *f* following the page number.

The manufacturer's authorised representative in the EU for product safety is Oxford University Press España S.A. of el Parque Empresarial San Fernando de Henares, Avenida de Castilla, 2 – 28830 Madrid (www.oup.es/en or product.safety@oup.com). OUP España S.A. also acts as importer into Spain of products made by the manufacturer.

www.ingramcontent.com/pod-product-compliance
Lightning Source LLC
LaVergne TN
LVHW011512200926
848484LV00001B/24

* 9 7 8 0 1 9 8 7 2 3 6 6 0 *